WRITERS AND THEIR WORK

ISOBEL ARMSTRONG
General Editor

MARINA WARNER

MARINA
WARNER

Laurence Coupe

NORTHCOTE
BRITISH
COUNCIL

First published in 2006 by Northcote House Publishers Ltd, Horndon, Tavistock,
Devon, PL19 9NQ, United Kingdom.
Tel: +44 (0) 1822 810066 Fax: +44 (0) 1822 810034.

British Library Cataloguing-in-Publication Data
A catalogue record for this book is available from the British Library

ISBN 0-7463-1112-5 hardcover
ISBN 0-7463-0998-8 paperback

Typeset by PDQ Typesetting, Newcastle-under-Lyme
Printed and bound in the United Kingdom by
Athenaeum Press Ltd., Gateshead, Tyne & Wear

Contents

Acknowledgements

The author and publishers acknowledge with thanks Marina Warner's assistance and co-operation in the preparation of this study; acknowledgements are also due to the publishers of her work.

Biographical Outline

1946   Born Marina Sarah Warner, 9 November, London, England; daughter of English father (Esmond, a bookseller) and Italian mother (Emilia, a teacher, née Terzulli). Educated at Les Dames de Marie in Brussels (1953–9) and at St Mary's convent in Berkshire (1959–63).

1963–7 Studies French and Italian at Lady Margaret Hall, Oxford, graduating with a BA in 1967 and an MA the following year.

1967–72 Works freelance in London (*Daily Telegraph Magazine*, *Vogue*, etc.).

1971   Named Young Writer of the Year by the *Daily Telegraph*.

1972   Marries William Shawcross, a journalist. (Son, Conrad, born 1977.)

1981   After divorce from first husband, marries John Dewe Matthews, a painter.

1986   Fawcett Prize for *Monuments and Maidens: The Allegory of the Female Form*.

1987–   Numerous academic fellowships and visiting professorships at various institutions, including Getty Centre (1987–8), University of Ulster (1994), Oxford University (2001).

1988   Commonwealth Prize for fiction (Eurasia) and Booker Prize shortlist for *The Lost Father*.

1995–6 Harvey Darton Prize and Mythopoeic Society Prize for *From the Beast to the Blonde: On Fairy Tales and their Tellers*.

2000   Rosemary Crayshaw Prize (British Academy) for *No Go the Bogeyman*.

2001   Nominated for Booker Prize and Impac Prize longlists for *The Leto Bundle*.

Abbreviations and References

AAHS   *Alone of All Her Sex: The Myth and Cult of the Virgin Mary* (London: Weidenfeld & Nicolson, 1976; repr. London: Vintage, 2000)

DE   *The Dragon Empress: The Life and Times of Tz'u-hsi, 1835–1908, Empress Dowager of China* (London: Weidenfeld & Nicolson, 1972; repr. London: Vintage, 1993)

FBB   *From the Beast to the Blonde: On Fairy Tales and their Tellers* (London: Chatto & Windus, 1994; repr. London: Vintage, 1995)

FMOW   *Fantastic Metamorphoses, Other Worlds: Ways of Telling the Self* (Oxford: Oxford University Press, 2002)

IDW   *In a Dark Wood* (London: Weidenfeld & Nicolson, 1977; repr. London: Vintage, 1992)

IE   *The Inner Eye: Art Beyond the Visible* (London: National Touring Exhibitions, 1996)

IMW   *Indigo, or Mapping the Waters* (London: Chatto & Windus, 1992; repr. London: Vintage, 1993)

JA   *Joan of Arc: The Image of Female Heroism* (London: Weidenfeld & Nicolson, 1981; repr. London: Vintage, 1991)

LB   *The Leto Bundle* (London: Chatto & Windus, 2000)

LF   *The Lost Father* (London: Chatto & Windus, 1988; repr. London: Vintage, 1998)

MB   *The Mermaids in the Basement* (London: Chatto & Windus, 1993; repr. London: Vintage, 1994)

MIHK   *Murderers I Have Known, and other stories* (London: Chatto & Windus, 2000)

MMA   *Monuments and Maidens: The Allegory of the Female Form* (London: Weidenfeld & Nicolson, 1985; repr.

	London: Vintage, 1996)
MMM	*Managing Monsters: Six Myths of our Time: The 1994 Reith Lectures* (London: Vintage, 1994)
NGB	*No Go the Bogeyman: Scaring, Lulling, and Making Mock* (London: Chatto & Windus, 1998; repr. London: Vintage, 2000)
RP	'Rich Pickings', in *The Agony and the Ego: The Art and Strategy of Fiction Writing Explored*, ed. Clare Boylan (Harmondsworth: Penguin, 1993), 29–33
SP	*The Skating Party* (London: Weidenfeld & Nicolson, 1982; repr. London: Vintage, 1992)
W	Marina Warner's official website: www.marinawarner.com

Anderson	Lindsay Anderson, *About John Ford* (London: Plexus, 1981)
Benjamin 1	Walter Benjamin, *Illuminations*, ed. Hannah Arendt, trans. Harry Zohn (London: Fontana, 1973)
Benjamin 2	Walter Benjamin, *The Origin of German Tragic Drama*, trans. John Osborne (London: Verso, 1977)
Blake	*The Complete Poetry and Prose of William Blake*, ed. David V. Erdman (New York: Doubleday, 1988)
Coupe	Laurence Coupe, *Myth* (London: Routledge, 1997)
Dante	Dante Alighieri, *The Portable Dante*, ed. and trans. Mark Musa (New York: Penguin, 1995)
Eliade	Mircea Eliade, *The Sacred and the Profane: The Nature of Religion*, trans. Willard R. Trask (New York: Harcourt Brace, 1957)
Eliot	T. S. Eliot, *Selected Prose*, ed. Frank Kermode (London: Faber, 1975)
Frazer	Sir James Frazer, *The Golden Bough: A Study in Magic and Religion*, abridged edition (London: Macmillan, 1922; repr. 1987)
Freud	Sigmund Freud, *Art and Literature*, Penguin Freud Library, ed. Albert Dickson, trans. James Strachey (London: Penguin, 1985)
Gross	John Gross, *Joyce* (London: Fontana, 1971)
Lyotard	Jean-François Lyotard, *The Postmodern Condition: A Report on Knowledge*, trans. Geoff Bennington and Brian Massumi (Manchester: Manchester University Press, 1984)

Ricoeur	Paul Ricoeur, *A Ricoeur Reader: Reflection and Imagination*, ed. Mario J. Valdes (London: Harvester Wheatsheaf, 1991)
Said	Edward Said, *Orientalism* (London: Routledge & Kegan Paul, 1978)
Tredell	Nicolas Tredell, 'Marina Warner', *Conversations with Critics* (Manchester: Carcanet Press, 1994), 234–54

1

The Dragon Empress,
Alone of All Her Sex **and**
In a Dark Wood

Marina Warner describes herself as 'novelist and mythographer' (W 1). The description may not do justice to her range of work, as short-story writer, cultural commentator, literary critic, journalist, pamphleteer, editor and interpreter of fairy tales, children's writer, dramatist, librettist, curator of exhibitions, documenter of icons, and so forth. But the conjoined terms, 'novelist and mythogapher', will certainly suffice as a means of getting our bearings.

Consider, firstly, what is implicit in the second of them. A mythographer is someone who writes about mythology, in its various manifestations – which will include narrative, symbol, belief, practice. In order to do a thorough job, that writer will need a sound knowledge of history, for myths get made in time, by specific people in specific social contexts. Warner's mythography is especially impressive for its historical sense, which often leads her to original and incisive insights, as we shall see. But the implications of the term go deeper, for Warner's interest in history is twofold.

On the one hand, she cannot resist a fascinating fact. This is not a matter of pedantry: rather, she wishes to demonstrate the importance of empirical documentation so that the theory of myth does not become too abstract or universalizing, as in the 'archetypal' tendency to celebrate mythology as the transcendent expression of timeless truth. On the other hand, she insists that what we call 'history' is more than a sequence of events and ideas: it is at root a narrative, as we know from its etymology

1

(Latin *historia*, 'story'), and so overlaps with myth (Greek *mythos*, 'story'). Imagination is the very stuff of history; we cannot understand ourselves or others without understanding the way we narrate our own and others' lives. The emblematic detail, discovered by documentation, only becomes vital because of the capacity to make connections, establish bonds, which are more – but not less – than material evidence. History is the story we make out of that evidence.

Which brings us back to the first of those conjoined terms: Warner is proud to call herself a 'novelist'. That is, she sees herself as a writer of fictions, an inventor of stories (Latin *fictio*, 'imagined creation'). It is the novelist's task to create narratives that help the reader find imaginative bearings in the historical world, and this may involve a certain audacity. But of course, audacity may take the form of re-creation. Warner, along with writers such as Margaret Atwood, A. S. Byatt and Angela Carter, has dared to rework ancient patterns of narrative, giving them new relevance, new immediacy, new life. When stories are retold, new possibilities of experience and expression are opened up; the way we live now is open to creative revision. For, as 'mythographer', she knows how much historical context is required for *mythos*, and how much mythic context is required for *historia*. Fiction is her means of mediating between myth and history, and so of realizing their subtle interrelatedness. Having understood as much, we may come to see that Warner's function as 'novelist' and as 'mythographer' is continuous: the distinction between fiction and non-fiction, arbitrarily applied in literary categorization, will take us only so far in appreciating her considerable body of work.

*****

In this connection it might be noted that Warner's first published book is a good example of an historical study of a career to which the cliché 'stranger than fiction' surely applies. *The Dragon Empress: The Life and Times of Tz'u-hsi, 1835–1908, Empress Dowager of China* (1972) is full of material which would stretch credulity even in a novel. This being an obscure subject for most readers of English fiction and criticism, a few facts might be in order. I say 'facts', conscious that the reputation of

Tz'u-hsi has proved unstable: there has been much disagreement as to whether she was actively evil or, rather, passively compliant in various crimes and misdemeanours. The author favours the former interpretation, which is what one might expect – and, indeed, hope for – from the 'very bright young journalist' and 'astonishing young author' praised at the time by the reviewers (quoted in the publisher's blurb in the paperback reissue of 1993).

So the brief biography we can distil from Warner's book runs as follows. Tz'u-hsi was born in 1835, when China was ruled by the Manchus. Ingratiating herself into the Forbidden City, she became a concubine of the emperor, Hsien-feng, and bore him a son. When the emperor died in 1830, her main rival amongst the court concubines disappeared in mysterious circumstances. Moreover, the widowed empress not having any children, Tz'u-hsi's young son became emperor, thus giving Tz'u-hsi enormous power, as she was effectively co-regent with the existing empress. This was a time when there was much call for reform and progress, but the newly appointed dowager empress was deeply conservative, determined to resist all change, while consolidating her power within the existing hierarchy. Tz'u-hsi took every opportunity to promote her own interests, and cared little for the condition of her country or its people. She lived a life of luxury, wasting resources and demanding that her every whim be indulged. For example, she used funds reserved for the navy to have an elaborate summer palace built. She demanded extravagant banquets of exotic dishes, and she accumulated innumerable jewels. She kept 3,000 eunuchs in her bower within the Forbidden City. All in all, Warner presents her as ruthless and corrupt, manipulating tradition and the imperial aura for the purpose of enforcing her rule.

However, the 'life and times' portrayed here cover also an era of change. When the young emperor suddenly died (and his widow, possibly prompted by the dowager empress, had committed suicide), all did not go according to Tz'u-hsi's plans. With the simultaneous death of her co-regent, she appointed her own three-year-old nephew, Kuang-hsu, as emperor, thinking to have secured stability. However, as Kuang-hsu grew up, he became increasingly interested in the project of modernizing China. He began reforming the military forces and the legal system, and he approved the development of railroads and other innovations. As if this was not bad enough, he dismissed hundreds of Manchu officials, and even planned to have the dowager empress herself removed from office. Hearing of this, Tz'u-hsi had her nephew imprisoned and his followers executed or exiled. Halting the modernizing impulse, she put all her energies into the resistance of foreign influence in China.

In this, she was at one with the spontaneous movement among peasant youths, known as 'Boxers' (because they believed manual self-defence was magically powerful, more effective even than firearms), to throw out all European businessmen and Christian missionaries. In short, they had the same aim as the dowager empress: they wanted to preserve the status quo. The Boxer uprising of 1898 alarmed the western world by virtue of its violence and savagery; but Tz'u-hsi approved, for she saw that, ignorant and contemptible as these youths might have once appeared to her, they were on her side. An international force comprising many thousands of American, British, French, German and Russian troops marched on Peking. The dowager empress and her entourage fled north, while the Boxer uprising was suppressed. The power of the Chinese court was diminished, with many officials being forcibly removed.

When Tz'u-hsi eventually returned to the Forbidden City, in 1901, she had shrewdly altered her political stance: now, she was in favour of Western-style reform, and began to advocate the reduction of Manchu privileges. There was even talk of introducing representative government. However, her gestures were empty, given that China itself was virtually bankrupt, and no financial initiatives were likely to be realized in the foreseeable future. Moreover, true to form, she arranged for the son of the imprisoned emperor's brother to succeed, trusting that she might have more influence over him. However, no sooner had she done so, and no sooner had the emperor himself died (possibly poisoned), than Tz'u-hsi succumbed to dysentery. She died on 15 November 1908 at the age of 73, having dictated 'her valediction to the empire over whose disintegration she had presided for nearly fifty years' (*DE* 225). Her assessment of her own reign suggested that her vanity and her capacity for self-deception prevailed to the end. Warner quotes Tz'u-hsi as follows: 'Looking back upon the memories of these fifty years ...

4

I perceive how calamities from within and aggression from without have come upon us in relentless succession, and that my life has never enjoyed a moment's respite from anxiety' (*DE* 225).

What is remarkable about *The Dragon Empress* is the ability of its young author to find a thread which will guide her and us through the labyrinth of nineteenth- and twentieth-century China. By tracing Tz'u-hsi's schemes and offences, she gives us a vivid sense of another world. That is not to say that Warner falls into the trap of what Edward Said will call, six years after the publication of her book, 'orientalism'. By this term, Said denotes the European image of the Orient, which it constructs as its 'other', and by which it defines itself. That is, the West maintains its identity by casting the East in the role of its own shadow – mysterious, exotic and sinister. This image, he proposes, has only served to justify the colonization and domination of the Orient (Said, 3). Warner's challenge, then, is to tell a good tale featuring a fascinating protagonist, and to do justice to the sheer weirdness of life in the Forbidden City, without caricaturing the East or misrepresenting the complexities of modern Chinese culture. Obviously, it is important to recognize her decision to take the rumours of Tz'u-hsi's extreme behaviour as nearer to the truth than are those apparently more neutral accounts which assume her to be guilty of weakness rather than wickedness. But then, the problematical nature of the relation between fact and interpretation is precisely Warner's concern. *The Dragon Empress* foregrounds the 'story' in 'history', and leaves the reader to make up her own mind. For history is not over and done with; and historiography is not a neutral exercise. This book brings both these ideas vividly home to us.

The Dragon Empress sold well when first published, in 1972, and again when reissued in paperback in 1993. But in retrospect, for those who know the rest of Warner's work, it may seem an odd choice for her first book. As she reflects in her 'Note on Rereading *The Dragon Empress*, 1993', it 'wasn't the first book I wrote, but the first I had published, because the subject – a wicked woman in power – was of interest to many people' (*DE* vii). As for her own motives in writing: 'Tz'u-Hsi drew me then for personal reasons, and some of these have now faded and indeed embarrass me. My interest in the culture of China still stands, but I am no longer looking, as I was then, for models of female authority. In that, I was in step with the feminism of the times. Heroines and leaders, rulers and fighters, regardless of intrinsic merit or ability – let alone virtue – were the necessary opponents of history as it was taught' (*DE* vii). Hence a female who had a reputation for malice had seemed nevertheless to merit attention, precisely because she contradicted the standard model of female subservience. A wicked woman was at least an example of female vitality, initiative and independence. With characteristic circumspection, the later Warner looks back on the earlier Warner with embarrassment, given what history – that is to say, contemporary western history, rather than the modern eastern history which is the subject of the book – has demonstrated: 'The events of the Seventies and, especially, the Eighties, revealed that women in power are not identical with women's interests' (*DE* vii). She points to the most obvious example: Margaret Thatcher, who discredited the idea that female influence in government would ensure compassion in general and concern for women's rights in particular.

But though Tz'u-hsi and Thatcher may have proved unfortunate as 'models of female authority', they hardly exhausted the topic of the representation and reputation of women. Warner had at least initiated an important project: one that was to occupy her for some time to come. That she made sure to dwell on the darker, more dangerous version of the story of the dowager empress was not simply in the interests of writing a lively book. She wanted to query the dominant assumption – the male assumption – of passivity as the paradigm of female perfection. This she did by documenting one of the most extreme refutations of it. However, the complexity of her field of research – women's image – demanded that she had to address the beatific as well as the demonic figure. So her next book was about the Virgin Mary.

*****

The audacious claim of *Alone of All Her Sex: The Myth and Cult of the Virgin Mary* (1977) is that there is a terrible paradox at the heart of Christianity. On the one hand, its founding spirit is egalitarian and non-discriminatory: it is centred on the radical idea of the incarnation, by which the divine fuses with the human, and 'the Word' walks on earth (for Christ is understood to be both God and man). On the other hand, it effectively represses the flesh and oppresses the female. For example, the stress on Mary's submissiveness and passivity has proved far from liberating:

> By defining the limits of womanliness as shrinking, retiring acquiescence, and by reinforcing that behaviour in the sex with praise, the myth of female inferiority and dependence could be and was perpetuated. The two arms of the Christian view of woman – the contempt and hatred evident in interpretation of the Creation and the Fall, and idealization of her more 'Christian' submissive nature – meet and interlock in the advocacy of humility for the sex. (*AAHS* 191)

Eve was created as Adam's inferior (made from his 'spare rib', as the feminist journal of that name ironically reminds us); Genesis further narrates that it was because of her weakness in the face of temptation (succumbing to the serpent's wiles and eating of the fruit of the forbidden tree) that humankind fell, being driven out of Eden. Thus, the very identity and status of woman is restricted from the start – within the founding myth, as it were. In that case, the female ideal, embodied in the Virgin Mary, will have to be one which avoids womanly assertion and carnal life. This 'second Eve' must be beyond the temptations of the flesh and must be the personification of humility. Warner is fascinated by the paradox at the heart of the faith: 'The ascetic strain in Catholic doctrine has struggled with its incarnational and life-affirming aspects for centuries marked by Pyrrhic victories on both sides. The Word made flesh was a positive and joyous statement on humanity's behalf, although Mary's virginity – the unnaturalness of Christ's birth – undermined it' (*AAHS* 236).

Warner has a keen eye for paradox throughout the book. Thus, she gives due weight to the curious phenomenon of Mary's being both humble and high, both meek and mighty. After all, she is 'Queen of Heaven', 'Our Lady' or 'Star of the Sea', even while she is represented as docile to the point of self-abnegation. But then, as Warner demonstrates, such apparent contradictions have hardly hindered the assertion of ecclesiastical dogma. The bare, doctrinal bones of the cult of Mary – or 'Mariolatory', as it is more exactly called – are set out by Warner in her prologue:

> Four dogmas have been defined and must be believed as articles of faith: her divine motherhood and her virginity, both declared by councils of the early Church and therefore accepted by most of the reformed Christian groups; the immaculate conception, sparing her all stain of original sin, which was proclaimed in 1854; and her assumption, body and soul, into heaven, which Pope Pius XII defined in 1950. (*AAHS* xxiv)

How did a figure who is scarcely mentioned in the four canonical Gospels, the few references all stressing her subordination, come to have such importance officially attributed to her? The author does not hesitate to draw the political inference: the proclamation of the power of the Virgin Mary has gone hand in hand with the assertion of the power of a church which claims to be the only true, legitimate beneficiary of the authority bestowed by Christ on Peter. Thus, the papal 'Bull' which declared Mary's 'immaculate conception' – confirmed, that is, that she was the only human being not to inherit the consequences of the Fall of Adam and Eve – was 'an important strategic move in the long battle of Rome against its detractors, and, once again, as with the cult of *Maria Regina* in eighth-century Rome, the interests of the papacy were bound up with the cult of the Virgin. It was only logical that Pius IX followed up the Bull of 1854 with another, in 1870, proclaiming the infallibility of the pope a dogma of the Church' (*AAHS* 237).

Such insights are typical of the constant connections that the book makes between doctrine and power. To give another example: 'It was during the twelfth century that the Virgin was first given her feudal title Notre Dame, Our Lady' (*AAHS* 153). That is, the praise afforded the Madonna cannot be disentangled from history, from the social hierarchy that obtained at the time that a particular title or attribute was honoured. However, the Catholic church presents her as 'a fixed immutable absolute, and the historical process that changes the character of the Virgin is seen merely as a gradual discovery of a great and eternal mystery, progressively revealed'. The assumption is that 'Mary did not become Mother of God at Ephesus in 43; nor was she assumed into heaven in 1950, when it first became an article of faith: these things always were' (*AAHS* 334). Thus, she knows that the icon she was herself brought up to revere, as a Catholic, is inseparable from papal authority and church politics. There are historical reasons why 'the myth and cult' grew.

'These things always were': while doing scholarly justice to the ecclesiastical intrigues, the author is more concerned with how the figure of the Virgin Mary became rooted in the collective mind, how it worked upon important needs. We may refute the dogmas, but it is impossible to refute the appeal which the ideal and the image have had on believers. *Alone of All Her Sex* is especially illuminating on the connection between an apparently timeless truth and the various tales that people have told in time, hoping to find a bond with the earth: 'The parallels between pagan and Christian mythology have been exhaustively discussed early this century by eminent anthropologists and historians, like Frazer, who saw the Christian atonement as the last version of the ancient sacrifice of the fertility god' (*AAHS* 208). It may be recalled that Sir James Frazer, author of the twelve volumes of a massive work of anthropological speculation, *The Golden Bough* (completed 1915), argued that the various gods of antiquity derived from a vegetation ceremony designed to ensure the growth of the crops. The acting out of the death and revival of the deity was thought to renew the cycle of fertility. As a rationalist, he had no qualms about including Jesus amongst these gods, with Easter being the appropriate spring festival of rebirth (Frazer, 345–61). Queried by later anthropologists, since it was based only on Frazer's expertise in classical studies and was not informed by any field work amongst the communities which he claimed to have maintained a residual fertility religion, *The Golden Bough* has nevertheless proved hugely influential on poets, novelists and literary critics. Warner is one such, though it should be said that her reliance on him is only intermittent.

However, here Frazer's cue proves appropriately promising. Warner proceeds to situate Mariolatry in the context of the various fertility goddesses of the ancient Near East: Isis in Egypt, Ishtar in Mesopotamia, Anat in Canaan. In each case a mate who is also a brother and a son is forced to endure violent death, followed by an equally drastic revival; and in each case the wife/ mother/sister follows her period of mourning by actively seeking to facilitate the moment of rebirth. Again, virginity is an attribute of each goddess concerned, despite her clear association with sexuality and fertility: Christian mythology is, it seems, not so exceptional in being given to the convenience of paradox. Warner traces the implicit parallel tactfully yet firmly. Here, drawing on the Roman writer Plutarch's account of the Egyptian god Osiris, she makes a specific comparison between Isis and Mary:

> in Egypt, the cult of Isis centred on the death of her spouse and son Osiris, for whom the goddess weeps bitterly before she triumphantly resuscitates him, using the Egyptian rites of embalmment and mummification she invented for the purpose. Plutarch has left us a full account of this Egyptian myth, which was recounted and celebrated every year at the autumn festival. Osiris is killed, and Isis, keening for her lost love, wanders the world in search of his body; when she finds it, 'the Goddess threw herself upon the coffin ... with dreadful wailing ...' Then, 'when she was quite by herself, she opened the chest and laid her face upon the face within it and caressed and wept.'
>
> The image of the goddess with the miniature mummy of the dead Osiris across her knees ... forms a diptych with the image of the goddess nursing Horus, Osiris' son, just as in countless Gothic and Renaissance treatments of the Pietà, the slumped body of Christ is disproportionately small and the face of the Virgin anachronistically young in order to recall, with tragic irony, the mother who once held a baby in her arms. (*AAHS* 208–9)

But the connections do not stop there, with Christian iconography. Warner sees the whole Bible as essentially mythic, emerging from the context of ancient Near Eastern ritual. In this, she may seem reminiscent of Frazer; but her insights are her own. Thus, she considers the significance of the Song of Songs, or the Song of Solomon, in the Judaic Bible – known to Christians as the 'Old Testament'. Here she discovers a prefigurement of Mary's role, not as mother but as 'bride of Christ'. This is the description of the early Christian church given by St Paul; it is also the epithet adopted by women entering into a Catholic convent to become a nun. Warner provides the mythic context:

> There was a long biblical tradition of nuptial imagery. The prophet Hosea, writing before 721 BC, came into contact with the Canaanites'

fertility cult and its central drama of the annual marriage of the god Baal to his sister Anat, consummated in order to unleash the forces of nature. Hosea, while remaining faithful to the monotheistic and patriarchal nature of the Hebrew God, boldly adopted this rich nuptial imagery of the rites of Baal to describe the relations of Yahweh and his faithless bride, Israel. (*AAHS* 123)

This background provides Warner with the material for the vivid picture she creates of the central relationship of the Old Testament: 'God and his earthly bride dance around each other, sometimes clashing violently, sometimes uniting in loving harmony' (*AAHS* 123). The use of Frazer's comparative method – tracing parallels across time and space to discover a common pattern of myth – helps her explain the highly erotic content of the Song. She quotes it to good effect:

'Let him kiss me with the kisses of his mouth ...' opens the poem, and from then on the luxuriant images of desire and longing, of exultation and the peculiar anguish of love palpitate ever more potently. ... 'He shall lie all night between my breasts' (Song of Solomon 1: 13). When he calls her, wooing her in the springtime, she says: 'For lo, the winter is past, the rain is over and gone; the flowers appear on the earth, the time of the singing of the birds is come ...' (Song of Solomon 2: 11). ... In similar strain he sings: 'Thy navel is like a round goblet, which wanteth not liquor: thy belly is like an heap of wheat set about with lilies' (Song of Solomon 7:2). (*AAHS* 125–6)

The sexual aspect of the material may, then, be traced backwards to the existing fertility myth and ritual of the lands surrounding Israel. But it may also be traced forwards, as it were, to the Christian, sublimated version of the marriage motif. Jesus's nuptial parables (such as that of the foolish bridesmaids) offer evidence for this, as does the culminating image of the apocalypse, given in the Book of Revelation, of the Messiah marrying his chosen bride, Jerusalem.

Warner traces all this, and indicates how highly charged Christendom is with repressed eroticism. She cites, for instance, the sermons of St Bernard of Clairvaux delivered in the mid-twelfth century: 'The antithesis at the crux of Christian thinking lies nakedly exposed in Bernard's use of erotic imagery. For, in his mysticism, one expression of love – carnal desire – disfigures the pristine soul, but another expression of love – the leap of the soul towards God – restores the primal resemblance. But both loves are expressed in the same language, which is principally drawn from that most languorous and amorous of the poems, the Song of Songs. On this tragic tension, Christian discipline flourishes' (*AAHS* 129). Significantly, there is one figure upon whom the saint relies in order to resolve the tension, rhetorically at least:

> The 'kisses of his mouth' become, in Bernard's sermon, the special symbol of the moment of ecstatic union. But such moments cannot be sustained, and remain mere promises of future bliss in heaven. Only one creature ever attained this perfection: the Virgin Mary. Assumed into heaven, seated at Christ's right hand, she becomes the example for every Christian of his future joy. (*AAHS* 129).

By drawing on sexual symbolism, yet by exempting Mary from its implications, a chasm is opened up between the ordinary woman, who is identified with the lower, carnal level of love, and the paradigm of female perfection, who is identified with the higher, spiritual level of love. Womanhood is simultaneously celebrated and castigated. Again, Warner is alert to the paradox – or, less neutrally, the sinister fallacy – upon which Christendom has thrived: 'The icon of Mary and Christ side by side is one of the Christian church's most polished deceptions: it is the very image and hope of earthly consummated love used to give that kind of love the lie. Its undeniable power and beauty do not heal: rather, the human sore is chafed and exposed' (*AAHS* 133). The 'myth of the Virgin Mary', to use the terms of the author's subtitle, is a narrative complemented by an iconography, various liturgies, numerous feast days, innumerable relics, periodic processions (for instance, the crowning of the may-queen) – in short, by a mode of worship – which, for all its beauty and dignity, has proved disastrous for women. The 'cult of the Virgin Mary', or Mariolatory, stands in need of constant critique and resistance.

As to Warner's choice of the word 'cult', it was Frazer who argued that myth and ritual are complementary. 'Ritual' is close semantically to 'cult', so it may be that she has his kind of theory in mind. But for her, it seems, the interest of 'cult' is rather wider. After all, the etymology of the word relates it to 'culture'. A mode of worship is inseparable from a whole way of life. One of the fascinating things about *Alone of All Her Sex* is its detailed documentation of the legacy of the worship of the Virgin Mary within the Christian centuries. In particular, she is interested in how the secular imagination has benefited from, but also influenced in turn, the central icon.

There are many examples of this in the book, but one of the most striking is her account of the achievement of Dante, who may be said to adapt the Christian myth in order to give scope for human initiative, without querying the notion of hierarchy which the term 'Our Lady' suggests. His monumental *Divine Comedy*, written in the early fourteenth century, depicts a visionary journey through three cosmic realms: hell, purgatory and heaven. The poet, lost in a dark wood, is guided by his Roman predecessor, Virgil, into the depths of the inferno, inhabited by the damned, up the purgatorial mountain, where sinners who have the hope of salvation are lodged, and so up to the earthly paradise, the garden from which Adam and Eve were expelled. There he meets his beloved Beatrice, whom he admired on earth before her untimely death, and who has inspired him ever since. It is she who encourages him to take the final stage of the journey, up to the heavenly paradise, where he is granted a vision of God, experienced as pure light, and understood to be 'the love that moves the sun and the other stars'. Warner is in no doubt of its importance:

> The *Divine Comedy* succeeded where other lesser Christian poets had signally failed: it synthesized the highest Christian ideals of fulfilment through love with the celebration of a living human creature, Beatrice. And the Virgin Mary emerges from the poem as the cornerstone of the architecture of the Christian salvation, the instrument of the Incarnation and the merciful intercessor for sinners, including Dante himself. But she does not substitute for human love. In this respect as in so many others, the *Divine Comedy* is a unique document... (*AAHS* 161)

The Provençal poets of the twelfth century, the 'troubadours', had developed the concept of 'love's ennobling powers', but had done so in such a defiantly carnal way as to challenge the divine order itself. Dante's vision was more comprehensive, more fully human and at the same time more fully Christian:

It was Dante's unique genius that he was able to achieve the reconciliation of this eternal quarrel between the body and the soul in the sublime synthesis of divinity and humanity that is Beatrice. Devoted as Dante shows himself to be to the Virgin, living as he did during the rise of her cult, he focussed his love on a mortal woman whom he had known, whose appearance, dress and manners were important to him, to whom he had spoken and who had, in life, exchanged smiles and conversation with him as she walked in the narrow streets of Florence. Beatrice affirms the grandeur and nobility of the created world, of the human attempt to reach, know, and love goodness. She is not the tool of defiance against a God who forbids earthly attachments, but the special instrument of mediation between earth and heaven. ...

The *Divine Comedy* is the drama of Dante's personal salvation, wrought by Beatrice. (*AAHS* 162–3)

It is hard to believe that anyone who could write in such glowing terms about this secular extension of Christian mythology would choose to live entirely without 'the myth and cult of the Virgin Mary'.

As suggested earlier, both these terms from her subtitle will be familiar to readers who know their Frazer. He it was who became most closely associated with the 'myth and ritual' approach to mythography. This is an approach which Warner might seem to subscribe to, by virtue of that subtitle. But, though she owes a broad debt to Frazer, as have many writers (from T. S. Eliot to A. S. Byatt), her approach to myth is distinct. At first glance, one might suspect that she owes most to Carl Jung, who was especially interested in the papal declaration of Mary's assumption into heaven, because it vindicated an essential human need for the archetype of the 'eternally feminine', whatever criticisms one might want to make of Catholic doctrine generally. But in her Epilogue, Warner refutes this idea by invoking another authority, one she invokes more than once in this book:

Under the influence of contemporary psychology – particularly Jungian – many people accept unquestioningly that the Virgin is an inevitable expression of the archetype of the Great Mother. Thus psychologists collude with and continue the Church's operations on the mind. While the Vatican proclaims that the Virgin Mother of God always existed, the Jungian determines that all men want a virgin mother, at least in symbolic form, and the symbol is so powerful it has a dynamic and irrepressible life of its own. Roland Barthes again pinpoints this process with crystalline clarity: 'We reach here the very principle of myth: it transforms history into nature.' (*AAHS* 335)

Warner is quoting from the translation of Barthes's *Mythologies,* published four years earlier. The gist of that volume – a collection of articles written over several years – is that myth is historical, but presents itself as eternal; thus, it confirms and consolidates the status quo. Myths need to be queried rather than revered: one should always consider whose interests they serve, before deciding their merit. Above all, they belong to their time, and can become outdated, redundant, irrelevant. This may seem particularly true of the Virgin Mary, concedes Warner:

> the reality the myth describes is over; the moral code she affirms has become exhausted. The Catholic Church might succeed, with its natural resilience and craft, in accommodating her to the new circumstances of sexual equality, but it is more likely that, like Ishtar, the Virgin will recede into legend. ...
>
> As an acknowledged creation of Christian mythology, the Virgin's legend will endure in its splendour and lyricism, but it will be emptied of moral significance, and thus lose its present powers to heal and to harm. (*AAHS* 338-9)

However, it should be noted that the conclusion which we have just partially quoted begins as follows: 'The Virgin Mary has inspired some of the loftiest architecture, some of the most moving poetry, some of the most beautiful paintings in the world; she has filled men and women with deep joy and fervent trust; she has been an image of the ideal that has entranced and stirred men and women to the noblest emotions of love and pity and awe'. It is only then that we read: 'But the reality her myth describes is over ...' etc. Thus, a long hymn of praise precedes the secular, sceptical qualification. It might, then, be worth differentiating Warner's mythography from Barthes's, just as clearly as she distinguishes her own interest in the Virgin Mary from Jung's. Here we could do worse than to invoke the authority of the philosopher Paul Ricoeur, who has devoted a large part of his work to speculation on the status of myth within modernity and postmodernity. He is interested in how myth survives, and more particularly how it continues to fascinate us even though we may consider ourselves to be thoroughly rational and secular, and so immune to its power. For Ricoeur, there is a meaning to myth beyond critique. He explains:

> The horizon of any genuine myth always exceeds the political and geographical boundaries of a specific national or tribal community. Even if we may say that mythical structures *founded* political institutions, they always go beyond the territorial limitations imposed by politics. Nothing travels more extensively and effectively than myth. Therefore we must conclude that while mythic symbols are rooted in a particular culture, they also have the capacity to emigrate and develop within new cultural frameworks. (Ricoeur, 488)

Again: 'The *mythos* of any community is the bearer of something which exceeds its own frontiers; it is the bearer of other *possible* worlds. And I think it is in this horizon of the "possible" that we discover the *universal* dimensions of symbolic and poetic language' (Ricoeur, 489). So it is that Warner has managed to recuperate 'the myth and cult of the Virgin Mary'. She has acknowledged and documented its ideological function in maintaining the church's hierarchy; she has lamented the disastrous consequences it has had for women during the long history of Christendom. It would be naïve to think that the icon could be revered uncritically, without awareness of its context and consequences. Yet once the critique has been made, it is possible to celebrate the rich, imaginative potential of Christian mythology, revealed to us so brilliantly by Dante. The figure of Mary will continue to be 'the bearer of other *possible worlds*', as Ricoeur would say.

Thus, it is worth noting Warner's comments in the preface to the paperback reissue of the work, which came out in 2000. Here she is explaining how she finally decided that this was a book she had to write. She was visiting Vietnam with her first husband, William Shawcross, who had been sent to cover the war for the *Sunday Times*. At the time, she was rereading the New Testament, and was surprised to find how little mention there was of Mary there; but she also visited the cathedral in Saigon, where she was struck by the extent or 'global reach' of her cult. Then, on a trip to a shrine to the Virgin outside Saigon, she encountered a bombing raid. Among the group fleeing the American attack was 'the naked little girl who became one of the most piteous icons of suffering in that war, and still is'. She is referring to the photograph that became probably the most famous taken in the course of the whole conflict. She goes on:

> Being there, which strikes me still as unbelievable, stopped me havering about writing. I'd thought of visiting the Holy Mountain in a spirit of levity, even disdain for the expediencies of belief. But encountering that bombing attack sobered me up, and it became necessary to try and understand more about the infinite complexity of suffering and consolation that religion confronts. (*AAHS* xvi)

So perhaps the lasting impression of *Alone of All Her Sex* is not the disenchantment of the lapsed Catholic, nor even the determination to situate Mariolatory historically. Perhaps it is, rather, the fascination with the power of mythology to extend and remake itself, even while admitting and exploring its ideological function.

*****

Warner's first novel, *In a Dark Wood* (1977), owes a good deal to her previous works of cultural history. The theme of the western understanding of the east, central to *The Dragon Empress*, re-emerges here: the main character, Gabriel Namier, is research-ing the diaries of a seventeenth-century priest who became resident in China. The novel dramatizes the conflict of cultures and it debates the merits of attempting to reconcile Christian and Chinese religion. Again, we are reminded of *Alone of All Her Sex* when Gabriel, himself a priest, has his researches inter-rupted by a request to investigate the claims of three girls in Sicily to have had visions of the Virgin Mary. This outburst of 'Mariolatory' leads him to question the quality of his own faith.

Of the two works of non-fiction, it is perhaps the latter which dominates this work of fiction. We have noted how important the poet Dante was to the argument of *Alone of All Her Sex*, and he is a strong presence here too. Though the poet is not alluded to directly, the title cannot help but remind the vigilant reader of the opening of Canto I of the *Inferno*, which is the first book of Dante's *Divine Comedy*: 'Midway along the journey of our life/ I woke to find myself in a dark wood,/ for I had wandered off from the straight path' (Dante, 3). It is important to recognize that this feeling of having lost one's way in life applies both to

17

Gabriel and to his brother Jerome, who is almost as central to the plot as his elder sibling. They are both well past the midway point of their journeys, and devote much of their time to regretting the paths they have taken. In Dante's epic poem, which we have already referred to as an imaginative revitalization of Christian mythology, the poet-protagonist is brought to realize and repent his errors, under the inspiration of the gracious Beatrice, and so is finally granted a glimpse of God's love. In the case of Gabriel and Jerome, however, there is no such possibility, as their world – the world of the intelligentsia of mid-1970s England – is sceptical to the point of cynicism.

Even Gabriel, who is a Jesuit priest, finds it difficult to keep 'the divine vision in times of trouble', as the poet William Blake would have it. His faith has become an aridly intellectual affair, plagued both by doubts about the divine and by doubts about his own humanity. Jerome, too, is jaded and cynical, worn out by his attempts to maintain literary standards as editor of a critical review, and by the failure of communication between himself and his wife. Thus, the brothers are seen to undergo parallel crises, while the possibility of redemption by love, divine or otherwise, is dramatized within an apparently unpromising context.

As the novel opens, Gabriel is on the point of completing his research project. Not only is he editing the diaries of the priest, but he is also writing his biography. Andrew da Rocha, the seventeenth-century Portuguese Jesuit, had managed to ingratiate himself into the court of the Chinese emperor K'ang-hsi, as director of the Bureau of Astronomy in Peking. Thus, he had succeeded in his enterprise by way of his scientific knowledge, which he saw as complementary to his own Christian faith. This larger question of the relation between rational enquiry and traditional religious conviction is also something that concerns Gabriel, as is the problem of whether the appropriation of one faith by another, demanded by the Christian notion of mission, is permissible or even desirable. The diaries he is editing report several important discussions between Andrew and the emperor on the nature of religion and on the structure of the cosmos, but as they proceed, we see the Jesuit's hope for establishing the Christian faith in China wane, when other priests arrive with less facility for compromise. He dies nine years before K'ang-hsi's prohibition of the teaching of Christianity and his expulsion of most of the missionaries. Andrew's experience only deepens Gabriel's own crisis of faith.

While Gabriel gets on with his increasingly perplexing researches, Jerome is in a predicament over his journal, the *Albion Review*. Unbeknownst to him, it has been funded by the Central Intelligence Agency of the USA. Now he is due to be exposed for corruption and for facilitating reactionary ideas in the pages of the *New Radical*. He feels himself to have been betrayed by his supposedly independent financial backer, and is angry that his high critical standards have been disastrously compromised. There is nothing he can do at this late stage; he has to face the fact that his literary life is virtually over. Meanwhile, his wife Teresa is preoccupied with her acting career, and is boasting about having a central role in an updated version of the musical, *South Pacific*, set in Vietnam. Contemptuous as he is of this gratuitous exploitation of an international disaster – the war waged by the USA against the Vietcong – he nevertheless stands up for his wife in a drunken argument after the opening performance. The husband of Francesca, one of their two daughters, is the war photographer David Clarke, who has recently returned from the conflict: he accuses Teresa and the rest of the company of being 'parasites', even 'scum'. Jerome's chivalrous gesture is perhaps as near as he will get to affirming any sense of affection for Teresa, and the novel suggests no inkling of a more profound marital reconciliation.

However, the larger theme of the novel is the chance of other kinds of reconciliation, filial and fraternal. When Gabriel's researches are interrupted by a request from the head of his order to travel to Sicily to investigate the claims of the three children concerning the Virgin Mary, Jerome's other daughter, Paula, proposes that she and her father should accompany him. Her dream is that love can overcome all differences. Paula is an artist, currently engaged on the task of illustrating a children's handbook of mythology. Since getting closer to her uncle, whom she has previously regarded as cold and arrogant, she has enjoyed debating with him the meaning of the ancient myths, including the biblical, and provoking him into conceding that there is an element of misogyny in many of them. Paula is herself looking for a feminine ideal, which might strengthen her

19

against the misery of the recent ending of a love affair. She is also intrigued by how Gabriel manages to maintain outward allegiance to his faith, despite his strong streak of rationalism. However, in Sicily, when all three are sitting together on the terrace of their *pensione*, a debate which she initiates on the nature and status of religious vision results in an unpleasant disagreement.

Paula and Jerome defend the idea of seeing the sacred in the profane, of finding the divine in the everyday world. Paula even goes so far as to propose that 'Each of us carries his own paradise inside him' (*IDW* 191). This visionary capacity would link her with Beatrice, and we might expect her to play the role of the mediator between earth and heaven here. But such declarations only annoy Gabriel, who arrogantly declares, by way of ending the discussion: 'You both speak about things you know nothing about, and I'd rather not discuss them' (*IDW* 192). This leaves Paula inclined to agree with an earlier judgement on their uncle, made by her sister Francesca: 'He's been a dried-up, juiceless bore all his life, pompous, conceited, tyrannizing everyone, Dad included, because of his great reputation, though God knows how he got it in the first place. ... He epitomizes for me everything that's sterile, that's the opposite of real or good' (*IDW* 105).

But little does either sister know how much Gabriel is suffering. Prior to this trip, he has met and become infatuated with a young musicologist, Oliver Summers, who specializes in baroque instruments and shares Gabriel's interest in the kind of mechanisms Andrew constructed. Oliver seems to welcome and encourage this interest, but Gabriel himself is plagued by guilt and self-hatred. His neat, rational framework has been shown to be vulnerable. Now, the experience of investigating the reputed apparition of the Virgin has brought home to him even more the aridity of his own world view. The eldest of the three girls, Maria Pia, turns out to be the illegitimate child of a local priest; her mother, treated callously by the church, is dismissive of the girl's claims. In his own way, and for his own reasons, Gabriel wants to dismiss them too. Indeed, he writes a report in which he explains away Maria Pia's vision as resulting from her being ostracized and living as an outsider, on the edge of the community; he infers also that her mother's 'morbid grievance' against the church has led her to think she has heard a denunciation of ecclesiastical practice from the mouth of Mary. In short, Maria Pia's vision is both her challenge to the society that has marginalized her and 'her attempt to be reintegrated at a higher level' (*IDW* 204). Rationally, this explains the matter; but spiritually, Gabriel knows there is something he has not properly understood. His intellectual power, his sophisticated theology, is insufficient to respond to the mysterious power of the events in Sicily:

> That evening he recited his daily Mass in a side chapel in the church. It was unattended, so he said it in the old way, in Latin, and some of the dryness left his soul till through the comforting and familiar patterns of the sacrifice he was able to reach once more a territory of the mind where he could scrape some water from the stony ground. (*IDW* 205)

This language of drought would seem to vindicate Francesca's judgement; but the novel gives us access to the *agon* which Gabriel is acting out. It is no coincidence that Paula is preoccupied with mythology: the very language here evokes the world of fertility myth, documented in so much detail by Frazer. The god and the land are as one; if the god lacks vitality, so too does the land; the god must die and revive if the land is to be renewed. And, indeed, Gabriel does die, after his return to London: driven to distraction by his sexual urges towards Oliver, and distraught when he discovers that a confidential letter he had written to the young man was left lying about while he went away on holiday, he wanders out onto the heath, hardly aware of where he is going or why. There he is accosted by two youths, who take him to be an ageing homosexual 'looking for trade' (*IDW* 235) Knocking him to the ground, stealing his money and running off, they leave him unable to gain his breath, and he dies where he falls. In Frazerian terms, we might see him as a dying god who is unable to complete the cycle of renewed fertility.

Yet the novel does not end on that tragic note. With Gabriel's death, Jerome and Paula vow to complete his editorship of the da Rocha diaries. Thus, the two brothers have at last been reconciled, and the young woman's desire that love should triumph has been fulfilled. In the Dantesque context, then, has

Paula taken on the role of Beatrice, effectively? The parallels are there, but the gap between the two personages seems intended to indicate the difference between an age of faith and an age of anxiety. That said, love does manage, if not to conquer all, then to provide some meaning and direction in the lives that remain. Paula at first blames herself for Gabriel's death, as she had recommended walking on the heath as a cure for his insomnia. But when Oliver visits Paula to return the Chinese prism which Gabriel had given him, she is released from her burden of guilt, because she realizes that it was the older man's infatuation that drove him to distraction and, indirectly, death. A kind of peace descends upon her. Moreover, she feels attracted to the younger man, as he does to her. The novel ends: 'She returned his kiss, but without closing her eyes, because she wanted to look at Oliver, and remember Gabriel' (*IDW* 246).

Thus, while we are not granted a fully Dantesque vision, we are asked to entertain the possibility of redemption. Gabriel's squalid death is placed within a larger pattern of affirmation. His spiritual struggle has not been entirely in vain: Paula, at least, will continue to dwell on the nature of vision, on the relationship between the sacred and the profane, and on the meaning of myth. In this last regard, the title of the novel has another resonance also, which we have hinted at earlier. If we shift our perspective back from Dante to Frazer, it surely evokes the celebrated first chapter of *The Golden Bough*, in which he describes the sacred grove of Nemi, where thoughout the period of the Roman kings, and right through to the decline of the empire, the fertility god was thought to dwell, in the personage of a man whose one certainty was that he was bound to meet a violent end. For, as impersonator of the god, his fate was to be killed by his successor, in order that the cycle of vegetation could begin again. Frazer invites us to

> picture to ourselves the scene as it may have been witnessed by a belated wayfarer on one of those wild autumn nights when the dead leaves are falling thick, and the winds seem to sing the dirge of the dying year. It is a sombre picture, set to melancholy music – the background of forest showing black and jagged against a lowering and stormy sky, the sighing of the wind in the branches, the rustle of the withered leaves under foot, the lapping of the cold water on the shore, and in the foreground, pacing to and fro, now in twilight and

now in gloom, a dark figure with a glitter of steel at the shoulder whenever the pale moon, riding clear of the cloud-rack, peers down at him through the matted boughs. (Frazer, 2)

This kind of romantic evocation is not echoed in Warner's prose; but it would not be inappropriate, perhaps, to see not only incidental motifs but also the basic structure of her novel as relying on the implicit paradigm of fertility myth, as documented in Frazer's work of scholarship. Both Jerome and Gabriel have entered into the autumnal stage of the cycle, but feel that their lives have been wasted. In the Frazerian model, the god's death is the necessary prelude to rebirth. So the novel may be seen to pose the question of whether a new beginning is implicit in their approaching end.

This theme is substantiated by the constant references to a literal wood – that on the heath, where Gabriel is to die. When, early on in the novel, he walks Paula home, she is prompted to ask rhetorically: 'The Romans were right to fear woods, weren't they?'(IDW 37). Frazer's sacred grove, in which the crucial *agon* between the present 'king of the wood' and his would-be successor takes place, is perhaps suggested here. Moreover, the figurative dimension of Warner's title is given further weight by Gabriel's nightmare, prompted by the guilt he feels for his infatuation with Oliver. It may not be fanciful to surmise that she has that first chapter of *The Golden Bough* in mind when she writes:

> Gabriel was dreaming. He was in a dark wood, and he was running. Brambles tore at his legs like barbed wire, branches of thorn trees grabbed his chest and gashed his cheek as if they were live hands reaching for him. They bore open, scented flowers in deceptive meekness, like garlands. The ground was steep and stony, it broke his feet through his shoes. Through the thatch of branches overhead the thin light spattered the ground crashing past him. He was finding it hard to breathe and his chest hurt, but he kept on running because behind him, he could hear four hounds giving chase. (IDW 116)

But even here, the Frazerian voice gives way to the Dantesque, as Gabriel reflects: 'The hounds of virtue were after him' (IDW 117). In Dante's poem, the poet's way is blocked by three animals, who are usually interpreted as representing three of the deadly sins; but these are no match for the hound who will be seen later in the poem, usually taken to signify Christ himself.

The allusions have been mixed here, but the extension of meaning from Frazer to Dante is evident. When the nightmare is realized, in a debased form, by Gabriel's death, we are not only to think of him as a displaced form of the dying god, but we are also to think of him as a Christian undergoing a redemptive sacrifice. Thus, when Paula kisses Oliver, we may think of her as the goddess mating with the reviving god, in order that the cycle may be renewed; but we may also think of her as representing spiritual possibility – a secular, bewildered but well-intentioned Beatrice, perhaps. This possibility is substantiated by Jerome's having quoted, after the argument over Teresa's musical, from the most famous of John Donne's sermons: 'No man is an island, entire of itself; every man is a piece of the Continent, a part of the main. ... Any man's death diminishes me. Because I am involved in Mankind; and therefore never send to know for whom the bell tolls; it tolls for thee' (*IDW* 231).

Thus, the structure of the novel moves, no matter how tentatively, from difference to identity, from discord to reconciliation, from enmity to love. In this sense, the structure is comic, in the same way as Dante's is: it begins with disunity and ends with unity. The same may be said of the pattern documented by Frazer within the vegetation myths of antiquity: there is a move through death to life, through sterility to fertility, through winter to spring. Perhaps the description of Paula in Sicily is apposite: 'Paula strode on to the terrace in a flowery dress cut for a woman three times her girth. She had bought it from a market stall, and her studied gawkiness made her floating frock, with its aura of matronly teatimes of gossip and complaint, seem a thing of wit and comedy' (*IDW* 175). The comedy may not be 'divine'; but in so far as love is affirmed and our faith in humanity is restored, the novel is strictly speaking comic nonetheless.

However, this does not mean that *In a Dark Wood* offers to heal the wounds of modernity with a few hints from Dante and Frazer. Within the structural impetus of the novel, there are difficult historical themes being negotiated. We have already raised these, when we noted the debt owed to the previous works of non-fiction. There is the question of the attitude to the East by the West, as is raised in *The Dragon Empress*. Andrew da

Rocha uses his knowledge of science to win the approval of the emperor, and hopes to persuade him that Confucianism, Taoism and Buddhism are compatible with Christianity. He succeeds, in that K'ang'hsi passes an edict granting tolerance to Christians in China, even though he lives to see his work undone. But Andrew is all along full of doubts about his enterprise: how far is he convinced that the wisdom of the Bible can be made compatible with the I Ching, and how far can he ignore the elements of irrationality and superstition in native Chinese religion when trying to reconcile it with God's Word? Conversely, we might say that the novel itself prompts the reader to speculate by what right a western religion can presume to rank eastern religions in a hierarchy of acceptability. The issue is echoed elsewhere in the narrative, not only by Gabriel's own speculations on the merit of the Bible, but by the Vietnam version of *South Pacific*: surely it is unethical to use the horrors of warfare as a medium for artistic indulgence. Though the author herself does not pronounce on this, the novel itself forces us to confront this issue of the morality of appropriation. The novel, that is, urges responsibility.

Similarly, we are invited to consider what is involved in Gabriel's own interpretation of Andrew's life and times. On the one hand, the two men are both priests; they share an interest in science, and particularly in mechanics; they are both seeking to justify their faith in a difficult situation. On the other hand, the gap of three centuries yawns between them, so that they inhabit, in effect, separate worlds. A main theme of *In a Dark Wood* is the question of the possibility of understanding the past in the present. This is indicated when Gabriel's state of excitement while engaged in research is described: 'he was the prisoner of a high and perfect state of subjectivity, so that all experience, however remote – even the seventeenth century in China – became meshed with the immediate circumstances of his life. He struggled to blot himself out so that he could feel once again the times and the man he was writing about. But he could not, and history became interwoven with his own imaginings' (*IDW* 120).

However, it would be a mistake to read the novel as a condemnation of subjective historiography. We know from our reflections on Warner's account of the Virgin Mary in *Alone of All Her Sex* that such a figure must come alive now or never. The task is not to explain her away, once and for all, but to understand her anew. For we are all involved in history, even as we write about it. Had the challenges faced by Andrew not mattered personally and deeply to Gabriel, his researches would have been thin and meagre. What the novel dramatizes is the dialectic between past and present: they are necessary one to another. Otherwise, history would be an irrelevance, and the past would truly be a foreign country. What matters, the novel implies, is that we take responsibility for the way we inherit the past, and the uses to which we put it. If we are responsible, we need not think of what is distant in time as remote from us in spirit. In that sense, we may speak, with the poet and critic T. S. Eliot, of 'the presence of the past' (Eliot, 38). This is a notion which Warner will pursue further in her next book.

2

Joan of Arc and *The Skating Party*

In the fifteenth century, during the Hundred Years War, a young peasant girl began to hear the voices of saints telling her to free France from the English and to help the Dauphin, Charles, to be crowned king. She made her way to the court at Chinon, where she convinced him of her sincerity; he gave her permission to don armour and to lead an army to relieve the city of Orleans. Having forced the English to raise the siege, she proudly attended the crowning of the Dauphin as Charles VII at Rheims. After this she defeated the English several times, but failed to take Paris. A year later, she was captured by the Burgundians, who sold her to the English. Accused of being a heretic and a witch, she was condemned to death and burned at the stake in Rouen. She was only 19 years old.

'A story lives in relation to its tellers and its receivers; it continues because people want to hear it again, and it changes according to their tastes and needs' (*JA* 3). That is how Warner begins *Joan of Arc: The Image of Female Heroism* (1981). She is perfectly conscious that Joan is primarily an historical figure, with an objective existence, well documented by the records of her trial and execution. Yet 'story' and 'history' are not, we should remind ourselves, antitheses. What interests Warner is how the myth of Joan grew up within the historical context of late-medieval France, and how the myth was developed and transformed in the succeeding centuries. Hence the book is divided into two parts. The first part is entitled 'The Life and Death of Jeanne la Pucelle': this is about the past, as interpreted in the present. The second part is entitled 'The Afterlife of Joan of Arc': this is about the present image of the martyr saint, as informed by layers of speculation and imaginative investment.

27

History and myth meet, just as do past and present: 'Joan of Arc was an individual in history and real time, but she is also the protagonist of a famous story in the timeless dimension of myth, and the way that story has come to be told tells yet another story, one about our concept of the heroic, the good and the pure' (*JA* 7). In this light, the author announces her intentions:

> To find out the reasons why she lodged in the minds of people who heard the story, so that it came to be told again and again until it passed into the collectivity of our culture, is a wonderful and gripping problem. By decoding the context in which she flourished – both of her own lifetime, when she was accepted by her own people, and of her posthumous fame, when she was described and reinvented by wave upon wave of new generations who adopted her – I want to make her real again. (*JA* 7)

But does not 'decoding' run the risk of emptying the myth of its power? Warner broaches this issue herself, when she admits: 'It is demythologising, perhaps' (*JA* 8). However, in restoring the mythic image to the historical sequence of event and aftermath, of interpretation and reinterpretation, Warner's book is meant to rescue Joan from a 'pristine and timeless' heroism and restore her to 'the soil of circumstance', to 'history's rich diversity' (*JA* 8).

Of course, the fact that Warner's topic is specifically 'female heroism' means she would be loath to abstract the heroic from the experiential. Her subject, as with *Alone of All Her Sex*, is the representation of a woman and the implications of that representation for women generally. What fascinates her about her chosen subject is that she destabilizes the ideology which confines, constrains and denies the female. Unlike Mary, this woman's appeal is her initiative, her enterprise, and her refusal to compromise:

> Joan of Arc is a pre-eminent heroine because she belongs to the sphere of action, while so many feminine figures or models are assigned and confined to the sphere of contemplation. She is anomalous in our culture, a woman renowned for doing something on her own, not by birthright. She has extended the taxonomy of female types; she makes evident the dimension of women's dynamism. It is urgent that this taxonomy be expanded further and that the multifarious duties that women have historically undertaken be recognised, researched and named. Like Eskimos, who enjoy a lexicon for many different words for snow, we must

develop a richer vocabulary for female activity than we use at present, with our restrictions of wife, mother, mistress, muse. Joan of Arc, in all her brightness, illuminates the operation of our present classification system, its rigidity on the one hand, its potential on the other. (*JA* 9)

As Ricoeur might say, it is by restoring the myth to history that we can actualize the 'possible worlds' which are contained within it, waiting for release.

Warner believes that, in order to trace the myth of Joan of Arc, we have to uncover the cultural context within which she emerged: this is necessary if we are to understand the extent of her challenge to convention. We have to be alert to significant details, such as her early choice of title: 'Jeanne la Pucelle'. Warner explains: '*Pucelle* means "virgin,"' but in a special way, with distinct shades connoting youth, innocence and, paradoxically, nobility. It is the equivalent of the Hebrew *'almah*, used of the Virgin Mary and the dancing girls in Solomon's harem in the Bible. It denotes a time of passage, not a permanent condition' (*JA* 22). Virginity being regarded by the medieval mind as magical, her chosen name carried all sorts of possibilities, which still resonate:

> With an instinct for seizing a central image of power, she picked a word for virginity that captured with doubled strength the magic of her state in her culture. It expressed not only the incorruption of her body, but also the dangerous border into maturity or full womanhood that she had not crossed and would not cross. In this sense she was a tease. During the whole course of her brief life Joan of Arc placed herself thus, on borders, and then attempted to dissolve them and to heal the division they delineated. In the very ambiguity of her body, which had to be shown to the crown to assure them she was a woman, in the name that she chose – which means 'virgin' and yet simultaneously captures all the risk of loss – she shows herself to span opposites, to contain irreconcilable oppositions. (*JA* 23)

Ultimately, as Warner intends to show, the audacity of Joan exceeded her age, even while she drew on its sexual lexicon.

The book has much to say about Joan's androgyny, her very ability to live on the border between identities. In this, she was again drawing on received wisdom, that of the Christian religion itself. Warner quotes St Paul: 'There is neither Jew nor Greek, there is neither bond nor free, there is neither male nor female, for ye all are one in Christ Jesus' (Galatians 3:28). However, this is an ideal which has rarely been realized: 'historically the Church has hardly borne it out, and among the stratagems its women members have used to overcome deep-seated prejudice have been virginity – the renunciation of sexual relations – and transvestism – the renunciation of sexual identity' (*JA* 148). The latter has traditionally been regarded as a perversion of nature, but Joan's adoption of male attire was in the spirit of Christian theology rather than the conventions of medieval Christendom. Warner stresses the radical aspect of her courage: 'That a woman contravened the destined subordination of her sex when she wore men's clothing underlies many of the prohibitions against it. Transvestism does not just pervert biology; it upsets the social hierarchy' (*JA* 147).

How oppressive that society could be is evident in its diagnosis and punishment of what it called 'witchcraft'. For Warner this is an index of its obsession with orthodoxy and its intolerance of spiritual independence:

> It was wedded to an ancient dualism, seeing an eternal contest between absolute good and absolute evil taking place perpetually in the world and in the microcosm of each person's soul; but such a cosy surface of absolutism was cracked by a deep relativism in the diagnosis and location of evil. The society was pain-wracked and haunted; it sought to pinpoint the nature and the place of evil, to find the person embodying it, because in an age when the patterns of thought have become anthropomorphic, it must be embodied. This attempt was like trapping mercury, for what seemed evil slipped away from the analyst's finger and thumb with maddening agility. The location most feared for evil's thriving was in the heart of heresy and of heresy's handmaid, witchcraft. Therefore, in a case like Joan's, it is often difficult to disentangle accusations of specific *maleficium* [harmfulness] from terror of general heterodoxy. The former is an effect of the latter, but often its most characteristic and revealing mark. Joan's cross-examiners concentrated on charges of minor sorcery because by implicating her in such activities, she would be naturally guilty of the more fundamental crime. (*JA* 101–2)

Joan's contemporary opponents, her late-medieval interrogators, could only deal with her by viewing her as an expression of pure evil. But her modern champions have also erred by going to the other extreme, idealizing and abstracting her so that she

30

becomes drained of the very life for which she is admired. For the Renaissance, she became a 'personification of virtue' (*JA* 218); for the nineteenth century, inspired by the ideals of romanticism, she became the 'child of nature' (*JA* 237). Most interestingly of all, in the late-nineteenth and early twentieth centuries, she was claimed by both church and state, both by the faithful and the sceptical. In her final chapter, 'Saint or Patriot?', Warner documents the competing interpretations, demonstrating how each presumed to have identified the 'true' Joan.

The central division of interest is vividly illustrated by a description of two statues erected in honour of Joan in Domremy, the village of her birth. In one, created by André Allar, which was erected at the entrance to the basilica in 1891, we see Joan being guided by the three saints who, she claimed, spoke to her:

> Joan, dressed as a peasant, kneels in an attitude of alarm and humility, one hand shielding her face, the other outstretched in wonder before her three voices, who are raised high above her on a brick wall and are cast in precious bronze in contrast to her white marble. Catherine holds out a sword, Margaret a helmet, and Michael, slightly higher than the others and spreading tremendous wings, raises himself to his full height, points with his index finger of his right hand toward heaven and holds aloft her cross-staff banner in his left. Joan here is God's humble instrument. (*JA* 255–6)

The fact that she was once condemned by the church for claiming to hear voices, and for presuming to have been directly inspired by heavenly forces, has been forgotten. Joan is now the embodiment of Catholic humility. By contrast, Antonin Mercié's sculpture, installed eleven years later beside the bridge, just across from the D'Arc house, shows her 'exultant and radiant':

> She is enfolded in the fleur-de-lys mantle of a queenly figure, who, wearing a pearl-embroidered coif on her looped hair, represents France in its medieval form, the fifteenth-century realm. With her help, Joan lifts to the sky an avenging sword. ... The statue refuses all divine associations for Joan's achievements: secular France, it says, provided the passion and the inspiration that guided her. (*JA* 255)

One of these Joans is the pillar of Catholic reaction; the other is the prophet of secular, socialist nationalism. Warner is fascinated by the fact that both coexist in the very region of her birth.

As she further notes, the question of Joan's symbolic identity has continually acquired new historical significance. Thus, it is taken for granted that Joan is a saint, but her canonization only occurred as recently as 1920, as a response to pressure from 'groups like the Action Française who wished the Vatican to make a firm stand against the rapid secularization of France and the spread of unbelief in the Christian world in general' (*JA* 264). Yet only a few years before she had also been taken up as a figurehead by the feminist cause. In England, Christabel Pankhurst, campaigner for the female vote, was known as 'the Maiden Warrior' and her supporters wore badges depicting her in the guise of Joan of Arc (*JA* 263). Joan has become, in effect, 'a heroine for all seasons' (*JA* 263). But Warner's conviction is that, if such appropriation is inevitable, it is our task to question whether a particular appropriative strategy is reasoned and responsible. One might have expected her to endorse the feminists' Joan, but she finds it necessary to point out an unpalatable fact: 'Although the women's suffrage movement had its roots in socialist principles of equality, some of the leaders, like Christabel herself, became associated later with right-wing opinion principally represented by the recruitment drives in World War I, which were shamefully militaristic' (*JA* 263). So we have to have a sense of history in approaching the Maid of Orleans, but we must be careful not to confine her to a specific historical cause. She will always transcend it, and offer her own challenge to it. The potential of myth can never be exhausted.

However, Warner also is at pains to point out the limiting effect of the supposedly transcendent image of Joan, as eternal victim. True, there will be those who, legitimately, find a parallel between Joan and the Messiah himself, in that her glory is bound up with her death as an innocent victim: 'Her stake is likened to Christ's cross: through it, her virtue can be transmitted to others and save them. Her perfection is preserved by her climactic end in violence, just as a goldsmith in the process of annealing heats the metal in the fire till it glows and then plunges it in water to seize all the heat's virtue, now transmitted to the gold, and uses them for his purpose' (*JA* 268). It would be foolish to deny the analogy. Again, others will think of ancient Greek myth, and will point to the story of Iphigenia who, as Warner reminds us, 'was laid on the altar of Artemis's rage, in order to lift the calm that prevented the Greek fleet's setting sail for Troy'. As with the Christian parallel, we see that 'Joan of Arc is a figure of sacrificial death, of redeeming goodness in its plenitude at the moment of its ceasing to be' (*JA* 268). But this recurrent image of 'Saint Joan', evident in countless representations – in sculpture, painting, theatre, poetry or film – is narrowly reverential. It seeks to contain the continuing challenge posed by the Maid of Orleans just as surely as do the various ideological appropriations mentioned above.

For, as Warner explains, the iconic status of Joan, as sacrificial victim frozen in time, forever young, has encouraged the view that 'what is desirable is unambiguous, firm, unchanging and intellectually retrievable from the seething flux of history and time' (*JA* 274). Warner's book, we recall, is an exercise in 'decoding', which involves the restoration of myth to history in order that its imaginative potential be released:

> By imposing accepted codification upon her uniqueness the figure of Joan herself becomes restrictive, another example of heroic virtue that confirms conventional notions of the heroic. Only by paying attention to her unique experience, and by acknowledging that it is at the same time universal, since the experience of every individual is unique, can the mould of received ideas be broken, and only when that mould is shattered can Joan of Arc escape from the confinement of order handed down from generation to generation into the splendour of the unaccountable, the particular and the anarchical. (*JA* 274–5)

It is only by subjecting the false idealization and abstraction of Joan's death to critique that we can grant her a rich, post-critical life. Political feminism may have been inspired by her image, but the more radical task is to resist the 'serious limitation' we have inherited: 'Because Joan of Arc is a woman, her story has been told within the terms of the available lexicon of female types, which is restricted. We are very inelastic in our mental attitudes and conform unknowingly all the time to conventional classification systems' (*JA* 274). The Joan of the future will be the androgynous figure who defies rigid categorization, rather than the Joan identified with any one idealization of her. 'She has been set up as a stable monolith in an unstable world, and yet all the different uses to which she has been put prove only the vanity of our widespread refusal to accept that it is impossible to trap the idea of virtue within boundaries that will not alter' (*JA* 275).

We ended our first chapter by referring to Eliot's notion of 'the presence of the past'. Warner's *Joan of Arc* might be said to illustrate this, demonstrating as it does the long and complex afterlife of Joan's image, and proposing as it does the possibility of a fuller, more humane interpretation which we should begin to make now. But it would be misleading to align Warner with Eliot too closely. Apart from substantial political differences – Eliot conservative and monarchist, Warner socialist and republican – their very conceptions of myth diverge radically. Eliot commends 'the mythical method' for writers as 'simply a way of controlling, of ordering, of giving a shape and a significance to the immense panorama of futility and anarchy which is contemporary history'. In short, it will be a step toward 'making the modern world possible for art', toward 'order and form' (Eliot, 177–8). One could not have a clearer contrast with Warner's faith that myth and history are mutually informative. The task proposed by the author is that of revealing the historical dimension of myth and the mythic dimension of history. It is in that sense that the past comes alive in the present: as unfinished business, as a question concerning our own conduct, as a persistent challenge.

*****

Order and disorder, myth and history, art and reality: these seem to be simple oppositions, yet we know they are not. Take, for example, the last of them: it is always tempting to pursue aesthetic perfection as a release from the contingencies of existence. But Warner wants to remind us all – artists included – of the cost of such a pursuit. Thus, at the end of *Joan of Arc*, reflecting on the way a painful, complex enterprise which ended in torment has been aestheticized in terms of serene sacrifice, she remarks: 'The disorder and formlessness of life are given shape by art; the limits of the work of art itself impose a structure that does not necessarily reproduce truthfully the circumstances of the subject; the mirror of art is faithless' (*JA* 269). Art of its very nature suspends the flux of contingent, confused life, in order to give it permanent form. Thinking of the iconic figure of Joan, she queries our desire for 'form' at any cost.

This is an important reflection to bear in mind when reading Warner's second novel, written shortly after her book on Joan, *The Skating Party* (1982). One of the central characters, Viola Lovage, is doing a postgraduate degree in aesthetics, and for the subject of her dissertation she chooses Gerard David's diptych, painted in Bruges, *The Judgement of Cambyses*. Her initial response is described as follows: 'At first glance, the painting seemed a traditionally gory, typically Flemish martyrdom. In the left-hand panel, the victim was lashed down, his face convulsed in agony, while an executioner sliced into the man's flesh with a knife, as if cutting out shoe leather to a pattern, and an assistant, knife between his teeth, parted the skin from the flesh the length of the man's raw and bloody leg' (*SP* 80). To one side stands a group of richly dressed, complacent burghers and their wives, while in the right-hand panel an imperial-looking figure looks on disdainfully from his throne. Viola sets herself the task of unfolding the story which the painting tells.

It is not what it seems, she discovers. Her first instinct is that one is supposed to feel pity for the victim, who appears to be 'the usual stalwart Christian' condemned by a pagan emperor, whom she takes to be the Cambyses of the title. However, her researches reveal that, in fact, Cambyses was a Persian tyrant, notoriously cruel, whose subjects rebelled and brought him to trial. It was decided that he should be flayed alive. Thus, Cambyses is the victim in agony in the left-hand panel, not the enthroned figure in the right-hand panel. Moreover, those standing by are painted from life: each one is based on a member of the town council of Bruges. It was these people who commissioned the painting, and who had asked that the face of Cambyses be based on that of a local judge recently found guilty of corruption. The painting is meant to symbolize the punishment which such offences deserve. Thus, Viola's first, pre-critical viewing of the work may need to be reconsidered.

However, on yet further reflection, she realizes that even the information she has discovered does not define or exhaust the meaning of the painting. It would diminish the artist's vision to see it as a justification of violence. So her first instinct was not so naïve: the horror at the central act, and the sympathy for the central image of extreme suffering, was not misplaced:

> 'Under modern eyes, *The Judgement of Cambyses* rises from its original, almost vulgar level of cautionary tale and becomes a fully articulated tragedy,' she wrote. 'The figures in the painting stir pity and fear at the human condition, at human presumption and human cruelty, regardless of the quarrels and vengeances that motivated the Town Council and were faithfully represented by David. With the lapse of time the violence in the painting has become grander in its implications, because it has been freed from the circumstantial grievances that inspired it, both in contemporary Bruges and in the Persia of the original source story.' (*SP* 83)

So, though art appears to arrest time, great art both expresses and exceeds the specific moment of its production. Indeed, it acquires meaning throughout history. Past, present and future exist in tension within it.

The Skating Party is, of course, itself a work of art. As a fictional work, populated by several characters who are capable of the kind of insights Viola has in the course of writing her dissertation, it is a particularly self-reflexive work of art. For example, no sooner has the central character made her conclusion on the painting, than we read: 'Viola had enjoyed herself hugely. Teasing out the strands of meaning hadn't been difficult, more of a game. But the idea of elucidating pictures until their ultimate meaning might be grasped had since become a passion, and she was now at grips with a far larger problem, a cycle of frescoes that had recently been discovered in the Vatican' (*SP* 83). We must return to those frescoes, but for now the implicit point should be registered: this is a novel in which the very act of understanding art is central, but which raises the question whether such an act, such a 'passion', can become yet another way of evading time, or responsibilities, or oneself.

Viola is the wife of Michael Lovage, a middle-aged academic, whose subject is anthropology. They live in a large house, Whitelode Farm, in a village outside his university town (which is strongly reminiscent of Cambridge). On the feast of the Epiphany, or 'twelfth night', Michael invites a few friends to skate along the Floe (or Cam?) from town to village, there to be served a meal. He and Viola are accompanied by their 17-year old son, Timothy ('Timmo'), who is much closer to his mother than his father, and who despises the latter's vague, liberal sentiments, preferring hard 'facts' and measurements. With them also is Katy, a classics undergraduate who is a year older: she is a striking figure, dressed mainly in black, and verging on the anorexic. She has an infatuation with Michael, which is reciprocated, though they have not consummated their affair.

Joining them are Jimmy Gattingley, an old friend of the family, and his young boyfriend Andrew. The latter has something in common with Timmo and Katy, namely an admiration for the work of a pop group called Crack; and he has the added interest to them of actually knowing the lead singer, Pete Razorblade. Completing the party is Professor Wilton, a reactionary figure who devotes most of his energies to resisting the advancement of female careers in the university. A contrasting character, whom we hear about but do not see, is Katy's tutor, Rowena Sidmouth, who has risen from humble origins to become a university don. She would seem to be everything Wilton is against. But Wilton's objections would seem to extend also, despite his being a friend of Michael's, to Viola: he cannot see the point of her engaging in academic research. It is against this background that Viola's determination to prove herself in the male academic world, and to outdo Michael intellectually, must be understood. Yet always, we sense her detachment: 'She was a watcher, who understood the act of looking on. That was why she liked painting, why she understood painters' (*SP* 9).

This group of characters is depicted skating along the frozen river on the morning of the Epiphany. This is the feast of the presentation of the infant Jesus to the gentiles, specifically the wise men who had travelled from the East to see him. Hence an epiphany is a manifestation of the sacred dimension in the profane world. James Joyce's early experiments in fiction were based on his theory of art as offering a secular equivalent of this: the profane suddenly becomes laden with symbolic significance, beyond its apparently trivial reference. As John Gross explains: 'An epiphany means a "showing-forth", and Joyce believed that if he transcribed a moment of revelation, however outwardly commonplace, with sufficient care, he could make it yield up its full spiritual value' (Gross, 34). In this context, we may note that Warner's novel does what she has said art inevitably does: it suspends time by imposing form on sequence. Indeed, in this scene her characters are almost literally 'frozen' in the moment, as are the figures in the winter scenes of Peter Brueghel the Elder. Like Joyce, she arrests lives that are trivial (no matter how highly some of these characters may think of themselves) in order to estrange them. We read: 'The skaters were moving like space voyagers in the void of whiteness ...' (*SP* 11). Again: 'their whirling, falling, swooping and giggling band seemed to trespass flagrantly against nature's white ceremony of stillness, and to desecrate the slow ritual of her winter pulse' (*SP* 87). But more importantly, the momentary scene is held up to view so that we may pause in order to let these lives assume their temporal identity, to let the past catch up with the present. By recognizing who people have been, we may come to know who they are.

Thus, Katy's admiration for Michael may seem incongruous, given his precious, knowing discourse. Like Professor Wilton and Jimmy Gattingley, he favours the smooth, self-congratulatory manner of speech, peppered with irony, which is obligatory in the academy. However, as the novel moves back and forth in time, we discover that he has an idealistic youth behind him. Indeed, Viola fell in love with him because she was impressed by his dedication to important political causes, notably nuclear disarmament. We are taken back to the day of a particularly violent demonstration, during which Michael showed considerable courage, though Viola – the inveterate watcher – found the event terrifying. But we see also how academic tenure and an increasing scholarly reputation modified Michael's idealism. Viola in time became increasingly disillusioned with him. The key episode is the field research he conducted on the island of Palau, accompanied by his wife and son.

We move back ten years, to witness a young female islander starving herself to death because she has been accused of witchcraft after another member of the tribe has fallen mysteriously ill. Viola, accompanied by the child Timmo, attempts to feed her, but in vain. To her amazement, Michael will not intervene: 'That girl is dying, and you do nothing'. But he has his justification, as anthropologist: 'In England, we're part of the social fabric; we are the society. Here we're intruders – our duties are different' (*SP* 102). The rituals by which the girl is judged, her victim cured, and the whole episode commemorated, are an object of academic enquiry; he wishes to keep the customs of the natives quite distinct from his own sense of morality and law. In a statement that is repeated twice in the novel (the second coming at the very end), he declares: 'Spells are binding only on the consenting' (*SP* 52, 180). But Viola makes her own reflection on the episode, which may be taken as a key to the novel as a whole. Regretting 'the part they had not played, their culpable non-participation', she comes to an awful realization: 'Blood is shed, she thought, and we are pilgrims in the temple of art who never smell its smell' (*SP* 141).

The spectacle of a young girl dying as the scapegoat of a society, condemned as a witch, inevitably reminds us of Warner's work on Joan of Arc. But we are reminded too of the speculations on art that arose from it. Viola's comment echoes Warner's own, which suggests that, despite her faults and limitations, she is closer to the authorial voice than is Michael. For his use of academic anthropology as a shield against the communal experience he presumes to document reminds us of how knowledge, once the idealism of youth has gone, may serve as a means of evading unpalatable truths. It is particularly ironic that Michael's complacent pronouncement – 'Spells are only binding on the consenting' – does not prevent him being spellbound by Katy. Her half-starved, child-like appearance, set off by her dramatically gothic dress, renders him helpless: his donnish dignity is vulnerable after all. Like the girl on Palau who literally does starve to death, Katy has the impact on him that the island's inhabitants might ascribe to a witch. So much for the wisdom and authority of the middle-aged academic.

The younger generation seems to sense that there is something lacking in the too-precious culture of its seniors. When Timmo, Katy and Andrew repair to the bedroom to listen to music, it is Crack which they opt for. Timmo plays one of his favourite tracks, 'The Big Mic Mac Machine', which is based on the kitchen routine in McDonald's:

> Take a burger out and flip it on the grill
> Leave it to broil while you're dipping in the fries.
> Go back to burger, turn it on its side
> Shake out the fries and tip them out to drain.
> Shove in the bun, scatter on the salt.
> Slice the bun in two, slip in the Mac. ...

> (*SP* 153)

This may strike any reader who is thoroughly inward with popular music as a caricature of an angry, punkish band. But it does enforce the question which the novel itself keeps asking: what is the function of art? Here at least is an art which savours of the real, oppressive, globalized economy in which most people have to live. It does not encourage detached, ironic contemplation.

There is an apparent contradiction here, perhaps. The novel is structured in three parts: 'On the Floe', 'The Frescoes in the Bathroom of Cardinal Birbarotti', and 'Whitelode Farm'. The short middle section is simply a description of the designs on the four walls of a bathroom constructed in the Vatican during the Italian Renaissance. These become Viola's object of study after the completion of her dissertation. The content puzzles her, and the novel hinges on her discovery of their hidden meaning. Like *Joan of Arc*, this is a work of 'decoding'. The contradiction to which I am referring, of course, is that Warner seems both to be criticizing the academic study of art, in so far as it entails an alienation from common experience, and to be basing her novel on the notion that high art really matters. The contradiction is easily resolved, however. *The Skating Party* is literary art, and it is about the problem of the aesthetic impulse. The rather ponderous account of the design on the east, south, west and north walls of the cardinal's bathroom is in fact a means of emphasizing the leap between past and present that has to be made if art is to come alive, and so to help us live.

For Viola, there seems to be no way into the story being told – or which she presumes is being told. 'The narrative remained impenetrable. No saint's life, no theological schema, no conventional cycle of the Passion or the Redemption or other Christian mystery could turn the key to the frescoes' meaning' (*SP* 86). Viola tries again and again to 'decode' the artefacts. Researches to discover the contents of the Cardinal's library have so far revealed nothing about any reading he might have done prior to commissioning the frescoes. One image in particular seems indecipherable: a woman imploring a youth. What does it mean? She makes herself a promise: 'When she found it, then her relationship as ignorant spectator would be altered, her role would develop another aspect, and like the twofold watchers of *The Judgement of Cambyses*, those inside the

40

painting and those outside it, she would become a participant in the drama the frescoes recounted' (*SP* 86).

Events on the feast of the Epiphany at Whitelode Farm fulfil her expectations. In the course of the skating party, she has come to realize how close Michael and Katy are, and her jealousy is aroused. In a brief conversation with Timmo, she finds herself putting it into his head that it would be a good idea for him to go to bed with the girl. Eventually, this is what indeed happens, and the two are discovered by Michael, who is followed hastily into the room by his friend. A non-Christian myth is evoked: 'Michael rubbed his burning eyes behind his glasses; he was amazed to find tears in them, and this sudden comprehension of his sorrow made him twist on Jimmy and hiss into his face, "He's my son, my son, and she ..."' (*SP* 168). The story of Oedipus has been reenacted, though now it is the father who is blinded. Michael's tears are a sign that the world has impinged upon his complacent milieu: he is tormented by a sense of desecrated family ties, and so has been made aware of 'the smell of blood'. But the mythic dimension of the action is wider still. Reflecting on the incident shortly after, Viola recalls that in her conversation with Professor Wilton he had mentioned Homer. She now sees that the mysterious image she has been dwelling on during her researches could make sense after all: 'Of course the *Iliad* was in the Cardinal's library, of course the frescoes told the story of a son who is cursed when at his mother's pleas he takes his father's concubine to bed' (*SP* 173).

Viola's task of interpretation would now seem to be at an end. The power of the past art work has become realized in the present. She has found herself able to participate in the contract of meaning. However, the question remains: how far has the 'smell of blood' actually entered into the 'temple of art'? Viola's interpretation of the Renaissance fresco depends upon her discovery of a text from antiquity. In other words, text is layered on text. Even the traumatic domestic event she has experienced is filtered through layers of culture. How do we know that the cocooned world of the Lovages has really been disrupted? The novel provides no answer. Rather, it allows Michael the last word, with which he simply repeats his earlier pronouncement: 'Spells are only binding on the consenting'. *The Skating Party*

41

remains ambiguous to the end. Even the most sympathetic figure, whom we might expect Warner to present as a decent woman trying to make her way in a patriarchal world, is seriously flawed. Not only does she effectively encourage Timmo's action, by way of getting her revenge on Michael, but her aesthetic studies are subject to the implicit critique made of the academy generally. One finishes the novel wanting the themes of the status of the female and of the function of art to be explored further by the author. That is what Warner does in her next work of non-fiction.

3

Monuments and Maidens and *The Lost Father*

Prior to the UK general election of 1983, the *Sun* newspaper carried the front-page headline, 'Vote for Maggie': it was urging its readers to re-elect as prime minister the leader of the Conservative party, Margaret Thatcher. This was accompanied by a depiction of her in the figure of Britannia. The image was intended to convey her patriotic commitment, as evinced by the recent victory in the Falklands, defending British territory against Argentinian claims. In the third chapter of Warner's *Monuments and Maidens: The Allegory of the Female Form* (1985), she considers the significance of the tabloid's choice of icon:

> The identification of the Prime Minister with the renewed military grandeur of Great Britain was accomplished in part through the language of female representation; it was natural, as it were, to see Mrs Thatcher as the embodiment of the spirit of Britain in travail and then in triumph, because of the way that spirit of Britain had been characterized, through its famous great queens on the one hand, and the convention of Britannia on the other. The first female premier did not rebel against the assimilation of the nation and herself; what Prime Minister would? For Britannia's image, developed through coins, banknotes, stamps, political propaganda and cartoons, has become synonymous with being British, with belonging to Great Britain. Any politician who can make her party seem inextricably entwined with the nation's identity, and any dissent from her views as unpatriotic, has achieved a notable propaganda success, however fallacious that popular impression may be. (*MMA* 43)

As with the various appropriations of the image of Joan of Arc which we noted in the last chapter, myth is seen to be inevitably implicated in history.

But as we have also seen, it is necessary to be wary of the way the present appropriates the past. Thus, it might be worth pondering the cultural roots of the 'popular impression' just mentioned. Tracing the origin of the figure of Britannia, Warner discovers that her image was first used on Roman coins, intended to depict the country Rome had conquered. It was only in the seventeenth century, with her reappearance on British coins in the reign of Charles II, that she acquired her present importance: 'Propaganda, marshalling supporters to one cause or another, became Britannia's chief theatre of activity. ... She was always [thereafter] associated with patriotism, especially after 1672, when the crosses of St George and St Andrew appeared on her shield. But her primary significance was the British constitution, her secondary, the pride that grows from the benefit it confers' (*MMA* 46). In the popular imagination, Britannia is often associated with the real historical personage of Boadicea, the British warrior queen of the first century AD, who raised a revolt against the occupying Roman forces. The fact that she was unsuccessful has not tarnished her impact. Warner notes how frequently both names were invoked during the Falklands crisis.

What, then, may we conclude about Margaret Thatcher's image? Warner speculates that 'in her, Britannia has been brought to life. But she achieved this singular hypostasis not because she is a battle-axe like Boadicea, but because she is so womanly, combining Britannia's resoluteness, Boadicea's courage, with a proper housewifely demeanour' (*MMA* 51). Though widely known as 'the best man in Britain', as she who 'wears the trousers', the 'conundrum' is that 'she never wears trousers': 'She is careful to live up to the conventional image of good behaviour in women prescribed for Conservative supporters. This image exists, like Britannia, in the realm of ideas; but Mrs Thatcher, both in reality and in iconography, surpasses the best Tory wife in Victorian domestic and female virtue' (*MMA* 51–2). Thus, we arrive at a general paradox about the representation of the female: a woman is conventionally chosen to personify an ideal, while most actual women are excluded from pursuing it practically. Mrs Thatcher is the exception that proves the rule; or, rather, we might say that her shrewd recognition that she ought to play the housewife, while holding national power, only illustrates the point.

Elsewhere, Warner reflects on the statues that adorn so many western cities: female figures embodying abstract principles. She generalizes in the light of the familiar iconography of the legislature and of government:

> Justice is not spoken of as a woman, nor does she speak as a woman in medieval moralities or appear in the semblance of one above City Hall in New York or the Old Bailey in London because women were thought to be just, any more than they were considered capable of dispensing justice. Liberty is not represented as a woman, from the columns in New York to the ubiquitous Marianne, figure of the French Republic, because women were or are free. In the nineteenth century, when so many of these images were made and widely disseminated, the opposite was conspicuously the case; indeed the French Republic was one of the last European countries to give its female citizens the vote. Often the recognition of a difference between the symbolic order, inhabited by ideal, allegorical figures, and the actual order, of judges, statesmen, soldiers, philosophers, inventors, depends on the unlikelihood of women practising the concepts they represent. (*MMA* xix–xx)

For example, the Statue of Liberty, erected in New York in 1886, stands facing the Atlantic and welcoming visitors to the United States. Its female character has always been intrinsic to its meaning. It soon became known as the 'Mother of Exiles', as is indicated by the verse inscribed on the plaque in 1903: 'Give me your tired, your poor .../Send these, the homeless, tempest-toss'd to me, /I lift my lamp beside the golden door!' (*MMA* 10–11). Warner comments:

> We are all her children, she speaks to us in the voice of a mother, as if responding to the entreaty of the ancient antiphon to the Virgin Mary, the *Salve Regina*: 'Exiled children of Eve, we cry unto thee, wailing and weeping in this vale of tears. So ... turn thy merciful eyes upon us.' ... The myth reverberates and the structure incorporates: when we visit the statue, and especially when we enter into her, we are invited to merge with her, to feel at one with her. (*MMA* 11)

But, despite the warmth of the invitation, the abstraction is what matters: 'Liberty is not representing her own freedom. She herself is caught by the differences, between the ideal and the general, the fantasy figure and the collective prototype, which seem to hold through the semantics of feminine and masculine gender in rhetoric and imagery, with very few exceptions'

(*MMA* 12–13). Warner is referring to the fact that in English, as in many other Indo-European languages, abstract virtues are habitually gendered feminine. For her, a good deal of historical struggle is hidden behind this apparently neutral linguistic information.

In order to see it, however, we need to view our civilization critically. This does not just mean that we are able to judge its faults, but also that we are aware that it has reached a 'critical' stage, where its continuing existence is in question. Warner is, in effect, saying that patriarchy would seem to have run its course, and she offers *Monuments and Maidens* as a contribution to its termination. In doing so, she invokes an impressive (male) authority. The epigraph to Part One, 'The Female Presence Today', is by the revolutionary cultural critic of the early twentieth century, Walter Benjamin:

> The course of history, as it presents itself under the notion of catastrophe, can really claim the thinker's attention no more than the kaleidoscope in the hand of a child, where all the patterns of order collapse into a new order with each turn. The image is profoundly justified. The ideas of those in power have always been the mirrors thanks to which the picture of an 'order' came about – The kaleidoscope must be smashed. (*MMA* 1)

This is the implicit impulse behind Warner's book, which is rather more uncompromising in tone than her previous works of non-fiction.

The element of cultural critique in *Monuments and Maidens* might, however, be occasionally overlooked by readers, there being such an accumulation of scholarly evidence. However, its radical agenda is present, right up to the end. The Epilogue consists of a brief meditation on the figure of Tiresias, familiar in antiquity: what, Warner wonders, can he teach us today? His story is simple enough. Seeing two snakes coupling, he strikes the female one dead with his stick, and as punishment he is turned into a woman; years later, seeing two other snakes coupling, he strikes the male one dead, and is turned back into a man. He therefore knows what it is to belong to both sexes. This dual knowledge goes with the gift of prophecy. Warner thinks his androgyny has itself proved prophetic, noting how strong a presence it is in the writings of such leading female novelists as Virginia Woolf.

She might also have mentioned the rich iconography of Joan of Arc, discussed in her previous work of cultural history. But here it is the relationship between androgyny and aesthetic practice that concerns her. She confirms the radical contribution of Woolf, who 'so rightly argued for the androgynous and protean mind of the writer, and wrote a version of the Tiresias myth in *Orlando*' (*MMA* 330). She is referring to the prose fantasy published in 1928, in which the protagonist changes sex even as his/her life spans five centuries. (It also includes a celebrated episode, set in the Elizabethan era, in which Orlando, as a young man, joins a royal group skating on the frozen Thames during the Great Frost: this may well be an influence behind *The Skating Party*.) This novel is probably the most adventurous work of English modernism. It inspires Warner to conclude:

> Biological sex cannot be the ring-fence in which the imagination lies wingless. Writers cleared it before painters; but visual representation, sculpted and painted, has continued to reify women in a manner some writers of fiction overcame some time ago, and mass communication of imagery has reinforced its limited code. ... But our vision is at last unclouding, and our ears are becoming unstopped and we are learning to see through the subject with her eyes and respect the individual inside the symbol. They have begun to speak from within, so many fantasy figures, Pandora and Eve and Tuccia and Liberty and Athena and other virgins, Justice and Temperance, and Lady Wisdom and naked Truth. Their voices are hoarse from long disuse, but they are gaining in volume and pitch and tone, they come to us from a long distance (their journey has been going on for more than two thousand years), and their limbs take time to move to the rhythm rising within, they have been subjected for so long. And they are saying, Listen. (*MMA* 333–4)

This utopian pronouncement has been hard won, given the scrupulous documentation which has preceded it. For she knows, as Benjamin knew, that the 'ideas of those in power' are resilient, and that the pleasure of the image of smashing the 'kaleidoscope' is inspirational rather than practical. There is a lot of painstaking work to be done, to which the cultural critic must contribute. Part of this work is the revision of an inherited vocabulary. Thus, in order for Warner to deal with the way the richness of female experience is reduced to an abstraction, she

47

has to reconsider the word 'allegory', featured in her subtitle.

We speak of art as allegorical when an image is intended to be translated into a concept. At the beginning of her book, Warner reminds us that allegory means 'other speech' (*alia oratio*): it 'possesses a double intention: to tell something which conveys one meaning but which also says something else'. This might seem a rather dry start, but she also adds: 'Irony and enigma are among its constituents, but its category is greater than both, and it commands a richer range of possible moods' (*MMA* xix). A little later, she promises that in her book she will explore the 'reverberating meanings' of female representations. Warner's book is not simply a critique of the various personifications of abstract principles that inhabit our cities; it is not simply about the way our culture gives itself away in phenomena that we either ignore or, if we see them at all, take for granted. In other words, it is not simply about ideology. The clue, I suspect, is in the notion of allegory expounded by Walter Benjamin.

Benjamin was interested in the traditional distinction – traditional since the Romantics, at any rate – between 'allegory' and 'symbol'. But whereas we have learnt to say that what chiefly distinguishes them is that the former conveys one meaning, while the latter conveys two or more, he looked at the former from a different angle. His famous definition runs: 'Allegories are, in the realm of thoughts, what ruins are in the realm of things' (Benjamin 2, 178). That is to say, where the 'symbol' claims to represent a timeless truth, which has supposedly found expression in the beauty of form, the 'allegory' brings attention to the transient, provisional nature of truth, which is evident in the fragmentary nature of modern experience. Within modernity, nothing is complete, and we are condemned to gesture towards wholeness, conscious that we can never attain it. However – and this point is equally important – it is imperative for Benjamin that we retain a sense of an absent plenitude of being, to which the allegorical artefact alludes. Thus, wandering among the 'ruins' of western civilization, like the nineteenth-century poet Charles Baudelaire's *flaneur* or idler, we may intuit the hidden potential of overlooked images.

Benjamin, who wrote a study of Baudelaire, also planned a research project on Parisian architecture. Warner herself devotes a whole chapter to a tour of the monuments of Paris, almost all female personifications. Despite her anti-patriarchal schema, her depiction of these is by no means negative. She works in accordance with Benjamin's idea of intuiting, beyond neglected artefacts or 'ruins', a richer, stranger meaning, tantalizingly just out of reach. Even as she dissects the ideology of the monument, she is on the look-out for 'signs and wonders'. She invites us to savour the continuing fascination of these sculptures, quoting Baudelaire for support: 'the stone phantom seizes you for a few instants and orders you, in the name of the past, to think of things which are not of this world. This is the divine role of sculpture' (*MMA* 19). The phrase 'not of this world' might be translated here as 'suggestive of another world'. The implication of the quotation for Warner, in the context of the larger invocation of Benjamin, is that public images may carry the promise of an alternative vision, even while they serve as embodiments of the status quo. That is, they may be utopian as well as ideological.

In this survey of iconography, there is one icon that stands out. Warner returns to it in more than one chapter. In doing so, she is not content to use it as one further illustration of her explicit theme. Indeed, she tries to demonstrate the rich potential of the image. It is that of Nike, the winged goddess of victory. We might do worse than follow her central account of this figure.

She begins by describing the high-relief carving created by François Rude for the Arc de Triomphe in 1831. This group sculpture 'celebrates the Departure of the Volunteers, the citizens' army, of 1792'; it is 'dubbed *La Marseillaise*, after the Revolution's marching song'. Dominating it is a figure of the winged Victory, which 'soars, sword to the fore, left hand upraised, huge wings unfurled, her torso plated in aegis-like scales, urging the men forward to victory' (*MMA* 127). The head is ferocious, like the legendary Gorgon. But Rude has 'adapted the imagery of vengeance and horror by combining it with one of the longest-lasting traditions in female allegory. The winged figure herself is a Greek Nike, a familiar cipher of Victory in the Western world and one of the mythological figures to survive almost without interruption from Greece to Rome to Christian Europe'. Moreover: 'Nike was an epithet of Athena: the goddess of the polis was the bringer of victory' (*MMA* 128). More exactly,

Nike 'acts as Athena's emanation, enhancing the goddess's might and stature by her hovering, often discreet, but always graceful presence' (*MMA* 129). The fact that she has no personality, no history, or that no story is attached to her, increases her power for personification by association:

> By the side of Athena or Zeus, she personifies the power they have to change human fortunes, and when she crosses the barrier from the divine universe into the human, she signifies that those fortunes have been changed for the best, for the person at whose side she stands or whose head she crowns, for the state on whose beaked ship she alights. She emanates from the immortals like a daimon, an aspect of their potency, and she passes into mortal experience to mark a moment when something changed. (*MMA* 130)

The complexity of Nike's function is indicated when Warner remarks upon a recurrent tension: 'she represents a power for whom speed is of the essence, yet who hallows and glorifies the spot of her temporary halt. This makes Nike resemble an aspect of time itself, or more precisely a way we see our relation to time' (*MMA* 133). Our normal experience may be stated as follows: 'Time and humanity are rarely at one, and language explores the separation' (*MMA* 134). We constantly feel ourselves to be dispersed in the flow of time, regretting the past and fearing the future. Hence the power of Nike's image: 'When she comes to a standstill in mid-flight over us she tells us that time now augurs well. And for a moment time's dread fails' (*MMA* 135).

Under the Romans, Nike was conflated with Fortuna, the goddess of fortune, with Fama (the goddess of Fame), and with what was called, as derived from the Greek, the *tyche* (the benign spirit hovering over a particular city). But, more interestingly, within Christendom, she was early on associated with the 'angel of victory' who acted as 'Christ's agent on earth' (*MMA* 138). The sex had changed by now, angels being conventionally male. But the imagery (a winged creature alighting above) and function (the bearer of good tidings) remained the same. The significance of this adaptation for Warner is, in general, that it allows her to present a more flexible thesis than her earlier pronouncements on gender stereotyping might have suggested. For her interest is not just in one aspect of female iconography, namely its oppression of actual women. No image, no myth, is ever static; and it would be to spoil a reasonable argument to disallow significant variations. Specifically, the transformation of Nike into angel allows her to digress on the nature of history; and, in particular, to reflect on the significance of Benjamin's contribution to our understanding of it.

She makes a bold claim for his general significance, and invokes him as a guide to the iconography she is describing:

> Walter Benjamin was this century's most acute critic of public lies and the culture of illusion. In 1921 he bought a small watercolour Paul Klee had painted the year before, entitled *Angelus Novus*. It hung on his wall in the different places Benjamin worked until, fleeing the Nazis, he left Paris, in June 1940. He returned to the image of the flying figure at different times in his writings. Through this wide-eyed creature of fantasy, who raises arms in surprise or even alarm, Benjamin meditated with profound sensitivity on the relation to the individual in his own times to fate and history and, perceiving in the image the ancient cluster of time's messengers – Nike-Fama-Fortuna-Tyche – he provides us with tragic testimony to the present century. (*MMA* 144)

Warner is deeply impressed by Benjamin's assertion of 'the need to accuse the old order, and bring destruction to the bourgeois culture which would culminate in the Nazis. The "new angel" hoped to vanquish it' (*MMA* 144). For almost two decades, he was able to see the winged figure as 'his *alter ego*', which was 'breaking up history to reconstitute it anew'; moreover, it was 'not itself subject to that destiny, but was in control' (*MMA* 144–5). Then the crisis deepened, and catastrophe enveloped him:

> In 1940, however, Walter Benjamin, writing in the last year of his life, before he left Paris and committed suicide, again turned to Klee's angel and invested the image now with the full tragedy he witnessed in Nazi Europe, as experienced by people like himself. Using the vocabulary of social advance that the Nazis had tainted with their propaganda, he re-created the former angel of promise as a doomed force for healing, no longer in command, but a victim like himself. (*MMA* 145)

These reflections prompt Warner to quote the celebrated paragraph from Benjamin's 'Theses on the Philosophy of History', in which he describes the angel as having his face turned towards the past, seeing the disaster of history all at once: 'Where we perceive a chain of events, he sees one single catastrophe which keeps piling wreckage upon wreckage and hurls it in front of his feet' (Benjamin 1, 259). Meanwhile, the angel himself is blown by a 'storm' into the future: 'This storm is what we call progress' (Benjamin 1, 259). Warner endorses Benjamin's insight into the Klee painting by stressing the complexity of the legacy of the past, as we bear witness to it in the present moment of crisis:

> In this remarkable ecphrasis of a small watercolour, Benjamin extends with tragic imagination the metaphor of time's halt implicit in the figure of the Greek goddess of victory. By describing the propitious angel blown off course and away, unable to command the movement of its wings, incapacitated by a greater force which forces submission, and therefore unable to stop in mid-flight, Benjamin dismantles unforgettably an image of coherence and control. He strikes at the centre of the crucial metaphor for security – the accompanying angel, epitomized by Nike, deliverer of good tidings – and conveys to us thereby most powerfully our shattered condition, our severance from happy days. (*MMA* 145)

Readers who embark on *Monuments and Maidens* expecting it to be a straightforwardly feminist indictment of the oppressive nature of iconography, soon realize that Warner is about more than that. True, this substantial work (over 400 pages long) does provide plenty of evidence of how personification has proved detrimental to female rights. But much of the work is taken up with this sort of speculation about the ambiguity of imagery, being at once ideological and utopian. A particular image may be rooted in oppression, or it may hold out a promise of deliverance. No image has a static meaning: 'allegory', in Benjamin's usage, indicates how the past has constantly to be recovered in the present, without any certainty of closure. Interpretation is always a matter of historical negotiation, tracing the clue of hope in the labyrinth of despair.

*****

The context of Benjamin's sombre meditation on the 'angel of history' was the triumph of fascism in Europe, which soon after led to his own death. This triumph is the background to Marina Warner's next novel, *The Lost Father* (1988). It largely takes place in Italy in the early decades of the twentieth century, and is in part a documentation of the malign influence on the country of the dictator Benito Mussolini. Focusing on the fictional region of 'Ninfania', located in the south of Italy, it bears witness to the gradual destruction of a way of life, the erosion of principles of conduct, the subversion of shared values. (It is worth mentioning here that Warner's own mother was brought up amidst the rise of Italian fascism, which almost certainly prompted her to write the novel.) Thus, the central character, a paternal figure who belongs to the old ways, is not only 'lost' in the sense that his early death leaves his family bereft, needing to cling onto the legend of his heroic end, but is also 'lost' in the sense that, while alive, he feels increasingly uprooted. With Benjamin in mind, we may say that Davide Pittagora walks among the 'ruins' of a culture, trying desperately to find meaning; and the members of his family, after his death, do likewise by idealizing him.

The Lost Father is not an easy read, given that the plot constantly moves between various pasts and the present. So it might be as well at the outset to give the story: that is, the rough chronology which underlies the subtle emplotment. We can do this by listing the significant dates to which the novel keeps returning. A simple sequence will save us a lot of unnecessary confusion, if we bear in mind that only the references to Mussolini are historically verifiable, and that the very first item concerning Davide is thrown into doubt by the rest of the novel:

1912   Davide Pittagora, a law student, fights a duel with his friend Tomasso Talvi, to defend the honour of his sister Rosalba (known as Rosa). A bullet lodges in Davide's head, and is unable to be removed.

1913   Davide, recently married to Maria Filippa, emigrates to the United States, taking his sisters with him. They have a difficult time surviving. But the sisters find the culture of free enterprise and economic opportunism more attractive than the quasi-feudalism they have left behind.

1919   Mussolini founds the Italian fascist party, dedicated to violent nationalism and the suppression of socialism.

1922   Mussolini becomes prime minister of Italy.

1923   The family returns to Ninfania.

1925   Mussolini becomes dictator of Italy, banning all

opposition parties a year later.

1931   Davide dies from lead poisoning, which is the result of the bullet lodged in his head.

1935   Mussolini invades Ethiopia. Davide's brother Franco stages an opera based on the story of King Solomon and the Queen of Sheba, designed to justify and glorify the invasion. It is poorly received by the audience, being too comical for the fascist cause.

In each of Warner's two previous novels, we have managed to make a link with the non-fiction she was writing prior to their publication. Thus, *In a Dark Wood* revisited themes explored in *The Dragon Empress* and *Alone of All Her Sex; The Skating Party* in some ways seemed to follow logically from *Joan of Arc*. In the case of *The Lost Father*, the desired connection is not immediately obvious. Yet, if we recall the main drift of the argument in *Monuments and Maidens*, it might be possible to trace a continuity of concern. Apart from detecting the presence of Benjamin in both works, we might also infer that some of the ideas contained in that study of 'The Allegory of the Female Form' are being dramatized here. In particular, we might think of Warner's suggestion that the construction of national identities in Europe has largely taken place by the restriction of women's rights in the process of personifying aims, ideals and principles through iconography. A strong nation has been always represented by an imposing female figure, even while actual women have found themselves demeaned and their activities restricted. Reading the novel, one's first impression might be that this thesis is contradicted, as we are introduced to a variety of strong-willed women. However, this strength is paradoxical, for what seems to be a female-dominated world, that of the fictional region of Ninfania, functions rather by virtue of the women dedicating themselves to the worship of the patriarch.

Historically, this is Mussolini himself, the brutal 'father' who wins over the women of the nation, persuading them even to surrender their wedding rings for the good of the fascist cause. Moreover, he has the power to rewrite history in the interests of self-aggrandisement. When he claims that a long-existing aqueduct has only recently been built on his instructions, there is an almost universal collusion in the deception, such is the depth and extent of fascist hegemony. The women especially want to believe he is 'the benefactor who had made water flow again in the south'. Thus: 'his way of loving his people rubbed out their knowledge, his touch erased their memory, like a burn which bites into the whorled skin and obliterates its pattern, until the victims' unique fingerprints can no longer be deciphered, and they can't recognise any more the shape of their hands or the marks they make, or keep faith with their memories or their history, but find all stolen away into the keeping of the torturer' (*LF* 185). The implications are profound: 'The Leader stole the old aqueduct for himself. It was only petty larceny, in the scale of all he stole, but in Ninfania it was a great matter. He wiped out the record of its construction, and provided another story' (*LF* 185).

In the context of the supremacy of the false, fascist father, Davide sees his world collapsing around him. Yet still he clings to his understanding of traditional lore, as he seeks to protect his wife and daughters from the squalor and brutality of the regime, all too evident to him in the course of his legal practice:

> Davide did not seek to change Maria Filippa's nostalgia for her idea of the past; his own old-fashioned style gave him stature and beauty to her eyes, he knew. Davide sheltered her, as a woman should be sheltered. If he could not haul the family out of their genteel poverty, he could at least protect his women, his wife and his daughters, from the knowledge that he and so many others shared, mute and unrecognised, in the offices of the law, in the architects' and developers' bureaux, in police and magistrates' waiting rooms, in prison office canteens, in teachers' common rooms, camps. You could keep it from the women, the hidden story of the cells and the cemeteries, of the club and the castor oil bottle. Everybody knew it, they knew it too, but if it weren't told, it could lose its power to injure. If it were quarantined, the contagion would stop. So he dreamed, so he resolved. How could he report to his girls the tortures he knew happened in the city prison? The bodies that disappeared into unmarked graves? Far better to leave them in innocence. (*LF* 117)

Nor had his earlier attempt at emigration to the States inspired him to consider that the old Italy might be better replaced by a bustling, brash culture of commerce. Applying for work on the construction of the subterranean train network in New York, he was met with a demonic vision, an 'inferno' in which men were 'bent like slaves to the yoke'; and all around, there was an atmosphere of 'depravity' which he felt to be degrading to his wife and daughters (LF 187–8).

So the truly paternal figure is Davide, husband of Maria Filippa and the 'lost father' of, amongst others, Fantina, whose memories of him are crucial to the novel's structure, since it is these that form the basis of the research and writing carried out by her own daughter, Anna. Davide, as the male focus of attention, is effectively the imaginative centre of the novel, even though he is absent (or 'lost') from much of it. At first, as we have noted, this kind of interest might seem remote from the thesis of *Monuments and Maidens*, which is about female iconography. Again, it might seem to counter the conclusions of the study of the Virgin Mary and the study of Joan regarding the mythologization of women. *The Lost Father* is about the mythologization of a man. Yet Warner's subtlety consists in showing us, in the story of how Davide's death acquires resonance in the lives of his wife, his daughters and grand-daughter, that the two processes are interweaved. Myth can constrain both sexes, even as it may appear to glorify one at the expense of the other:

> In death, Davide was enshrined; Maria Filippa brought up her daughters in the reflection of his wishes, and they could no longer be challenged; now that he lay on the narrow shelf in the family vault, transformed by prayer into an icon, he was more deeply imbued with the sacred mana of paternal power than ever the man Davide Pittagora had been when he was alive. (LF 192)

As Rosa reflects later: 'Stories are good for forgetting' (LF 202). This is a conundrum which Warner seems to want the reader to ponder.

For the novel is not confined to the past nor to 'Ninfania'; it is also about the perpetual presence of both. In London in 1985, we see Anna reading out part of the memoir she is writing on behalf of her mother Fantina, who has long since emigrated from Ninfania to England, having married an Englishman. As she reads, Fantina responds. She tries to assess whether Anna has captured the flavour of southern Italy in the early decades of the century. She tries also to decide whether her own memories, which form the basis of Anna's work, along with some diaries of Davide, are entirely reliable. This question of the relation between the event and the act of narration, between fact and fiction, between myth and history, is the central concern of Warner's novel. As Fantina will remark to Anna towards the end: 'I don't know any more where your book ends and my life begins' (*LF* 273). Moreover, Anna's job consists in the collecting and cataloguing of the ephemeral products of contemporary culture: toys, novelty items, cereal boxes, and so forth. Her writing-up of her mother's memoir, centred on the grandfather she never knew, who inhabited a world she finds it hard to imagine, might be seen as her own attempt to find stability and meaning in her life. A divorced, single parent who has been disappointed in her experience of men, she emerges in her narration as a bewildered figure, desperate to connect to a tradition, and to affirm some sort of continuity.

The crux of the story she is writing is the duel that her grandfather is supposed to have fought in the Ninfanian village of Rupe in 1912. The veracity of the event is in doubt, in that all the reports of it are part of the legend that has grown around it, thanks to the women's determination to revere his memory as an old-fashioned patriarch, dedicated to ideals that have since been eroded. The belief is that the duel was fought after he discovered that his sister Rosa had been sexually compromised by his friend Tomasso Talvi. As we read in Anna's text, based on Fantina's recollections, Davide was 'called by a distant, ancient summons issuing from the dimness of Ninfania's code of conduct' (*LF* 130). But the very 'dimness' of this 'code' means that it is difficult to relate the recent past in which Davide lived to the distant past of antiquity. Where do his roots lie?

It might appear that we are given some hint in an episode that takes place when Davide is 15 years old: he and his friend Tomasso search out an ancient villa that has recently been discovered, because the latter believes the frieze on one of its walls to be of particularly salacious interest. It depicts a group of women in a state of abandonment, cavorting before a phallic symbol. His friend savours the spectacle, believing it to indicate the true state of the female: 'This is women's business,' he declares, and adds that it was the women who 'did for' the Roman empire. Davide, however, is perturbed by the 'sacred mysteries' depicted: at first he cannot make out what is happening, and has to have the 'orgy' explained by Tomasso. Having been told, he cannot reconcile the sight with the reverence which he has been brought up to feel for women, and finds it hard to countenance the idea of their innate wantonness. Tomasso embodies the machismo of the Ninfanian culture in his view of the female as driven entirely by carnal impulses; Davide embodies the chivalric aspect, dedicated to the cult of the Virgin Mary (who is a constant referent in the novel). If these two will later fight each other, in the duel over the honour of Rosa, which of them will express the ancient 'code of conduct' more exactly? Perhaps both of them do.

Thus, we come back to the problem of interpretation. Just as Davide finds the frieze difficult to comprehend, so does Anna find the duel. If the past survives into the present, what happens to it? Is the past necessarily distorted, by making it conform to the assumptions of the present interpreter? If one is not native to the culture one is trying to understand, how does one know that one is being sensitive to its subtleties? These questions are pressing in the case of Anna, who is two generations away from Davide (he is born in 1893, she in 1950), and who only knows Ninfania through the medium of Fantina's reminiscences. Again, we have to pose yet another difficulty: what are the motives of the person engaged in reading the text of history? Thus, when Anna is translating the diaries for inclusion in the memoir, she reflects: 'Would Davide, my Italian grandfather, have appreciated this migration of race memory, of the spirit of the southern patriarch into the voice of the English grand-daughter? He was so lost, I wanted to fill up the emptiness. And yet, I wonder, would he have preferred silence?' (*LF* 192).

Her motivation is dramatized towards the end of the novel, during a trip to the United States, after a meal with Fantina and her sisters in 'Fun City', Parnassus. She keeps overhearing snippets of conversation about the past, and she feels again 'as I had as a child, when, eavesdropping from the landing in pyjamas, I had only been able to make half-sense of the grown-ups' chatter'. This in turn prompts her to make a resolution: 'I had to find a story of my own. I had to be able to give my account of the world ...' (*LF* 263). But this only begs the question of how far her own identity depends upon her interpretation of the family narrative. The meal has taken place in a tacky restaurant called 'The Old Pasta Pub', an absurd pastiche of the culture and the cuisine which Davide would have revered. It is all show; but then, is Anna not also engaged in constructing a drama out of the fragments of the past? She addresses her aunts in an interior monologue:

> My theatre stands in Ninfania, my old found land, harsh white with limestone shining in the sun, and wound in the shrouds of an ancient wisdom and its customs. I can see through you all in the Pasta Pub, through the microwaves and the air conditioning and the TV packs, I can put you back in my position on my toy stage, where my grandfather is gallant and gentle and as much a victim of the prevailing code as you, the womenfolk, the custodians of the family name. He carries a scar of honour and writes with an elegant hand, he sings baritone like plain chocolate melting in a copper pan. This is the place I want to be, I told myself. This is my family romance. (*LF* 265)

The Freudian resonance of that last phrase should not escape us. We are to infer that the daughters and the granddaughter of Davide have had an emotional investment in the memory of 'the lost father'. Anna, emancipated as she has tried to be, remains spellbound by a 'romance' which she unconsciously wishes to perpetuate, despite her professional concern for veracity.

She admits as much in the depths of the dilemma posed by the emergence of some evidence concerning Davide's death that throws the legend of the duel into doubt. A newspaper report of 1912 refers to a clash between the landlords' henchmen and a coalition of workers and students: 'Several participants were seriously wounded, including one student of law, who had assisted with the declaration of demands' (*LF* 270). Fantina and her daughter discuss the implications, with Anna being far more devastated by the revelation than is her mother. The likelihood is that Davide did not die in defence of an ancient 'code of conduct' but because of his involvement in contemporary politics: thus the event upon which she has been building the narrative of the memoir is probably false. Fantina tells her: 'You take things too seriously. ... But it's an old story. Old stories change, you know'. To which Anna retorts: 'But where did the duel idea come from in the first place? I thought it was *true*. I took it as something that had happened. God, I've been trying to write a memoir, based on *fact*, not a teen romance' (*LF* 274). Her mother's advice is that, as there is no way of deciding either way, it is better to leave the story as it stands; and this is what she does.

In the above riposte Anna protests rather too much, of course. She has already used the word 'romance' to describe what she is writing – though the distinction between the 'family' and 'teen' variants might merit a digression, if only space would permit. The larger issue is the more interesting one, however: the degree to which we believe what we want to believe, regardless of the evidence. Coming to the end of *The Lost Father*, the reader might be reminded of John Ford's cinematic meditation on the myth of the Wild West, *The Man Who Shot Liberty Valance* (1962). At the end of the film, one man is credited with killing the ruthless, violent villain, even though it is another man who actually did it. According to the editor of the local newspaper, this does not matter: one should always 'print the legend' (Anderson, 182). The film explores what this involves. Similarly, the novel alerts us to the implications of Anna's complicity with her mother in preserving the legend of the duel.

When Mussolini 'wiped out the record' of the original construction of the aqueduct, and 'provided another story', he demonstrated that the lie could become the truth. The point was to persuade the people to accept the new 'story'. *The Lost Father* may be seen as an interrogation of the responsibilities of storytelling. Mussolini is exposed as irresponsible – dangerously so. In the instance of the legend of the duel, judgement is less easy to make. For one can see why Fantina would want to retain a story that had served the memory of Davide well. One can see also why her daughter would concur. But Anna's decision is, I think, meant to give us pause for thought. What is at stake is the suppression of politics. The novel itself is rich in documentation of the effect of fascism on Italy, with its savage exaggeration of the existing machismo of a patriarchal culture. It prepares the way for this by documenting also the poverty and corruption of the years preceding the emergence of Mussolini. Yet the narrator of the family memoir finally chooses to suppress the probability that the man who has been so revered for so long on account of his remaining aloof from political struggle, preserving the chivalry of better times, chose to side with the workers against the landowners. Thus, for all she knows, he may have been quietly engaged in resistance to fascism, between his return from the United States until his death. Certainly, when Franco stages his sycophantic opera, we might want to ponder the contrast between his pragmatism and his late brother's principles. But all this is speculation, and the author remains silent. What we can say is that the ambitious scope of the novel, its inclusive historical sweep, places in perspective the account which Anna decides to write, making the very nature of interpretation an urgent concern.

Thus, if the relation between the fascist 'father', Mussolini, and his nation is a 'family romance', then we have to ask ourselves whether another kind of man is preferable. In Riba in 1933, Fantina, her sisters and their mother recall Davide's way with words:

> 'Yes, he was an orator,' said Maria Filippa.
> 'Like the Leader,' said Imma.
> 'Beh.' Maria Filippa's mouth turned down and she shook her head. 'Your father was shy, you know. He couldn't talk if he didn't want to, only among friends. Otherwise he wrote it down for others to speak.' She paused. 'There was something noble, something lordly about him, to my mind. Not like the Leader.' (*LF* 175)

The Lost Father asks us to consider what it means to be noble in an era of crisis. Heroism, it suggests, is not always manifest in the form of legends. Yet we cannot ignore the process of mythologization, for history is about rather more than 'facts'. We might say, in terms that Walter Benjamin would have appreciated, that the novel is an 'allegory' of absent meaning, which the story of the duel can only hint at. Comprehensive as it is as an account of patriarchy, fascism and the nature of cultural identity, it does not offer closure. It leaves the reader all too aware of the 'storm' that buffets the 'angel of history'.

4

From the Beast to the Blonde and *Indigo*

One of Walter Benjamin's most famous essays is 'The Story-teller', a celebration of the fiction of Nikolai Leskov, which he published in 1936. Benjamin's argument is that the traditional oral tale represented a 'community of listeners', with the teller of the tale existing in close proximity to his audience. What was heard was the voice of experience, which was highly valued. There was a wisdom implicit in the very act of narration: 'After all, counsel is less an answer to a question than a proposal concerning the continuation of a story which is just unfolding. To seek this counsel one would first have to be able to tell the story. ... Counsel woven into the fabric of real life is wisdom' (Benjamin 1, 86).

Now, he reflects, the story has been replaced by the novel, just as a predominantly oral culture has been replaced by a print-based culture, and wisdom has been replaced by information. This is something we should understand, for it is part of the process of secularization which we call modernity, and which pervades our lives. The novel is a literary, contrived attempt to offer a substitute for the moral authority of the directly narrated story. It cannot rely on community, but functions by means of indirect communication from one individual, the author, to another individual, the reader, who is unknown to him. 'A man listening to a story is in the company of the storyteller; even a man reading one shares this companionship. The reader of a novel, however, is isolated, more so than any other reader. (For even the reader of a poem is ready to utter the words, for the benefit of the listener)' (Benjamin 1, 100). However, it might just be possible for the writer in a secular, literate age to recapture the power of storytelling, if he has retained knowledge of, and respect for, the community which sustained it. At any rate, Leskov is a writer who, according to Benjamin, has retained the power of the story, and is able to transcend the alienation of print.

One of the more interesting proposals of this essay is that there is a particular kind of story which is formative of the whole genre:

> 'And they lived happily ever after,' says the fairy tale. The fairy tale, which to this day is the first tutor of children because it was once the first tutor of mankind, secretly lives on in the story. The first true storyteller is, and will continue to be, the teller of fairy tales. Whenever good counsel was at a premium, the fairy tale had it, and where the need was greatest, its aid was nearest. (Benjamin 1, 102)

As one might expect, Marina Warner includes a reference to Benjamin's essay in the first chapter of her monumental work, *From the Beast to the Blonde: On Fairy Tales and their Tellers* (1994).

But it is not this last insight which she invokes. Indeed, given her undoubted admiration for his thinking, it may surprise us that the allusion is so brief. However, it is in reading this book that we realize that her stance towards Benjamin is ambivalent. Anyone expecting this book to be an elaboration of 'The Storyteller' will be disappointed. For what she seizes on in that essay is its confusion over the nature of the 'community of listeners' to whose disappearance it draws attention:

> Benjamin never once imagines that his storytellers might be women, even though he identifies so clearly and so eloquently the connection between routine repetitive work and narrative – storytelling is itself 'an artisan form of communication,' he writes. And later, again, it is 'rooted in the people ... a milieu of craftsmen.' He divides storytellers into stay-at-homes and rovers – tradesmen and agriculturalists, like the tailors and shoemakers who appear in the stories, on the one hand; on the other, the seamen who travel far afield adventuring, like the questing type of hero. He neglects the figure of the spinster, the older woman with her distaff, who may be working in town and country, in one place or on the move, at market, or on a pilgrimage to Canterbury, and who had become a generic icon of narrative from the frontispiece of fairytale collections from Charles Perrault's onwards. (*FBB* 22–3)

Nor is hers solely an ideological objection – a feminist demand for the balance to be redressed in favour of the female.

Important as such a demand is, Warner is saying something else besides: she is indicating the very essence of the act of storytelling, which Benjamin, despite the brilliance of his insight, overlooked: 'Spinning a tale, weaving a plot: the metaphors illuminate the relation; while the structure of fairy stories, with their repetitions, reprises, elaboration and minutiae, replicates the thread and fabric of one of women's principal labours – the making of textiles from the wool or the flax to the finished bolt of cloth' (*FBB* 23). The word 'texture' is etymologically close to 'text': while not stating this explicitly, Warner is able, by emphasizing the 'weaving' of a tale by 'old wives', to move easily from the female teller of the oral culture to the female editor or author of the print culture. Though Benjamin's interest is more in praising Leskov than in damning modernity, that praise depends on the notion of a clear divide between spoken storytelling and written fiction. It is such distinctions that Warner wants to query, or at least revise: 'The relation between the authentic, artisan source and the tale recorded in book form for children and adults is not simple; we are not hearing the spinsters and the knitters in the sun whom Orsino remembers chanting in *Twelfth Night*, unmediated. But the quality of the mediation is of great interest' (*FBB* 23).

For from the mid-seventeenth century, 'the nurses, governesses, family domestics, working women living in or near the great house or castle in town and country existed in a different relation to the elite men and women who may have been in their charge, as children' (*FBB* 23). As houses were run with more brisque efficiency, and as children came to be more dominated by newly intrusive mothers or newly promoted governesses, those same children took refuge with their nurses or nannies, now displaced. The old 'rapports' created in childhood came to 'shape the matter of the stories' as they were written down when some of the children reached adulthood. Thus: 'the cultural model which places the literati's texts on the one side of a divide, and popular tales on the other, can and should be redrawn'. For 'fairy tales are an airy suspension bridge, swinging slightly under different breezes of opinion and economy, between the learned, literary and print culture in which famous fairy tales have come down to us, and the oral, illiterate, people's culture of the *veillée* [evening in company];

and on this bridge the traffic moves in both directions' (*FBB* 24).

Though the birth of the literary version of the fairy tale is credited to Charles Perrault's collection of 1697, his female contemporaries deserve as much credit, which Warner sets out to give:

> Women writers like Marie-Jeanne L'Heritier and Marie-Catherine d'Aulnoy mediated anonymous narratives, the popular, vernacular culture they had inherited through fairy tale, in spite of the aristocratic frippery their stories make at a first impression. Indeed, they offer rare and rich testimony to a sophisticated chronicle of rights and wrongs and ways to evade or right them, when they recall stories they had heard as children or picked up later and retell them in a spirit of protest, of polite or not so polite revolt. These tales are wrapped in fantasy and unreality, which no doubt helped them entertain their audiences – in the courtly salon as well as at the village hearth – but they also serve the stories' greater purpose, to reveal possibilities, to map out a different way and a new perception of love, marriage, women's skills, thus advocating a means of escaping imposed limits and prescribed destiny. The fairy tale looks at the ogre like Bluebeard or the Beast of 'Beauty and the Beast' in order to disenchant him; while romancing reality, it is a medium deeply concerned with undoing prejudice. Women of different social positions have collaborated in storytelling to achieve true recognition for their subjects: the process is still going on. (*FBB* 24)

In the same year as *From the Beast to the Blonde*, Warner collected six such stories – one from Perrault, five from his female contemporaries – in a volume entitled *Wonder Tales* (1994). An inference one may draw from the balance of contents is that the fairy tale – or, more accurately, 'wonder tale', since not all of them include fairies – is a predominantly female form. Beyond that, its capacity for infinite adaptation is a reminder that, even when it became literary, it retained the collective quality of the oral culture, incorporating its resourcefulness. At the end of her study of the form, Warner quotes her friend, Angela Carter, herself a supreme storyteller:

> Ours is a highly individualised culture, with a great faith in the work of art as a unique one-off, and the artist as an original, a godlike and inspired creator of unique one-offs. But fairy tales are not like that, nor are their makers. Who first invented meatballs? In what country? Is there a definite recipe for potato soup? Think in terms of the domestic arts. 'This is how I make potato soup.' (*FBB* 418)

Beyond that again, the example of Carter substantiates Warner's claim that a retold fairy tale can subvert patriarchal assumptions, can liberate women from generations of stereotyping.

All these ideas are implicit in that simple statement: 'This is how I make potato soup.' The sense of tradition as improvisation, as tactical variation on an inherited model, is important for Warner because the main aim of *From the Beast to the Blonde* is to restore the fairy tale to history, to rescue it from the abstraction of much modern interpretation. A prime culprit is psycho-analysis, which Warner rather incongruously identifies with the 'archetypal' approach to fairy tale. One might think that she had Carl Jung in mind, given his theory of the 'archetypes of the collective unconscious', which he regarded as eternal and natural rather than historical and cultural. But Jung scarcely gets a mention, and her main ire is directed at the Freudian reading of fairy tale – in particular, Bruno Bettelheim's *The Uses of Enchantment*. For instance, if 'Cinderella' is based on the opposition between the absent, good mother and the present, wicked stepmother, Bettelheim decides too readily that the meaning of the tale is child-centred. For him, the tale is about the child's desire to split off the desirable from the undesirable in the course of its emotional development, without feeling any guilt about its animosity towards the parent. Warner objects:

> This archetypal approach leeches history out of the fairy tale. Fairy or wonder tales, however farfetched the incidents they include, or fantastic the enchantments they concoct, take on the colour of the actual circumstances in which they are or were told. While certain structural elements remain, variant versions of the same story often reveal the particular conditions of the society which told it and retold it in this form. The absent mother can be read literally as exactly that: a feature of the family before our modern era, when death in childbirth was the most common cause of female mortality, and surviving orphans would find themselves brought up by their mother's successors ... (*FBB* 213).

In short, a story has an historical context as well as an archetypal content: perhaps it is even more interesting, if we would only take the time to consider it.

So what do we find if we cease to focus the fairy tale on the child protagonist, and take account of the narrator? Do we abandon Freud's 'family romance' – that anguished account of how children come to terms with their parents – altogether? Well, we certainly find a complex domestic scene, and we certainly find difficulties of emotional adjustment, but with Warner's mode of interpretation we make a significant expansion of perspective. In doing so, we find that the subtext of the tale may not be child-centred at all, but may involve 'bitter, internecine struggles between women'. For the narrator may be using her narration as the occasion to promote her own cause:

> If the storyteller is an old woman, the old wife of the old wives' tale, a nurse or governess, she may be offering herself as a surrogate to the vanished mother in the story. Within the stories themselves, the narrator frequently accedes symbolically to the story in the person of the fairy godmother. Mother Goose enters the story to work wonders on behalf of her brood. Good fairies are frequently disguised as hideous and ragged crones in order to test the heroine's kindness ... Even when the fairy godmother is described in less disparaging terms, the perception of sympathy between storyteller and fairy need not be set aside; the claim reflects the wish-fulfilment of the storyteller herself as understood by her audience and disseminated through the printed versions of the tales; in 'Donkeyskin' [in which the female protagonist is faced with the threat of incest with her father after the demise of the mother], the fairy helps the heroine to overcome the dangers her foolish/wicked mother has landed her in by her deathbed demand [that her husband should only marry someone more beautiful than herself]. (*FBB* 215-16)

Thus, though we know that the preponderance of dead or absent mothers in fairy tales reflects the real condition of widespread mortality through childbirth in early modern Europe, this is not enough to explain the amount of emotional investment on the part of the original narrators. We need to know a little more about the complexities of domestic life which revolved around marriage, mortality and remarriage. Warner, refusing to hunt archetypes for their own sake, given that the historical circumstances are fascinating enough, is effectively saying that sometimes the stories are about adult ordeals rather than childish wish-fulfilment. They will, of course, be about more than that – but they will not be about less.

Not that any of the above should be taken to imply that Warner is setting out to offer a simple justification of female behaviour. Rather, as the following observation will indicate, she is interested in the conflict between women within a patriarchal framework:

> If the narrator / good fairy is bidding to replace the mother whose death she announces in the story, if she is offering herself as the benevolent wonder-worker in the lives of the story's protagonists, she may be reproducing within the tale another historical circumstance in the lives of women beside the high rate of death in childbirth or the enforced abandonment of children on widowhood: she may be recording, in concealed form, the antagonism between mothers and the women their sons marry, between daughters-in-law and their husbands' mothers. The unhappy families of fairy tale typically suffer before a marriage takes place which rescues the heroine; but her situation was itself brought about by unions of one kind or another, so that when critics reproach fairy tale for the glib promise of its traditional ending – 'And they all lived happily ever after' – they overlook the knowledge of misery within marriage that the preceding story reveals in its every line. The conclusion of fairy tales works a charm against despair, the last spell the narrating fairy godmother casts for change in her subjects and her hearers' destinies. (*FBB* 216–17)

It will be clear from this imaginatively historical approach that Warner is not impressed by one of the main premises of modernist literary theory: the notion that the original intention of a work is irrelevant. In her second chapter she declares: 'Just as history belongs to the victors and words change their meanings with a change of power, stories depend on the tellers and those to whom they are told who might later tell them again. "Never trust the artist. Trust the tale," D. H. Lawrence's famous dictum, fails to notice how intertwined the teller and the tale always are' (*FBB* 25). If we are to understand the tensions which have given rise to female utterance, we have to know about the circumstances of women.

With regard to those circumstances, Warner concentrates mainly on the socio-economic context of the early modern period, as it was within this that the genre of fairy tale arose, but in the course of her argument she ranges more widely than this. For instance, an important female experience within Christendom generally has been that of being effectively silenced. Given the biblical depiction of Eve as bringing about the fall of humankind by both her willingness to succumb to demonic rhetoric (the wily serpent's verbal temptation to eat the fruit of the tree of knowledge) and her own formidable powers of persuasion (getting Adam to follow suit), women have been all too often associated with false language. The word 'gossip', which originally referred to a female friend invited by a woman to the christening of her child (a kind of godmother, significantly), had come to mean by the seventeenth century 'a woman who delights in idle talk'. Warner demonstrates how, in this very same period, women came to rebel against their submission, and used the narration of fairy tales as a mode of resistance. The opposition between silence and speech was central to the power of the story: hence the number of motifs of forbidden utterance and of the pronunciation of magic charms (*FBB* 29ff).

But where did the idea of the old wife claiming verbal authority come from? In a fascinating exercise in scholarly conjecture, Warner traces the role of the narrator back to the ancient figure of the Sibyl, the prophetess who continued to speak even though reduced to physical decrepitude. In youth she had agreed to sleep with Apollo only if he granted her wish to live for ever; but she forgot to ask for continuing youth, so that she was condemned to pine away in her cave without the release of death. Yet she continued to claim 'sovereignty' and to tell her truth to those who would listen. In Ovid's *Metamorphoses* she declares: 'By my voice I shall be known'. Quoting this, Warner comments: 'The voiceless who voice their "sovereignty" against the odds are by no means always female. But the blocked-up cave is unblocked in the imaginary world of her story, by the memory of her presence inside, the fantasy of her magic and knowledge' (*FBB* 11). The Sibyl became a model for the early narrators of fairy tales, condemned as they had been to silence and oblivion. As such, she continues to inspire all those who have been denied their rights:

> Stories often described as fairy tales, be they told in the Caribbean, Scotland or France, can flow with the irrepressible energy of interdicted narrative and opinion among groups of people who have been muffled in the dominant, learned milieux. The Sibyl, as the figure of a storyteller, bridges divisions in history as well as hierarchies of class. She offers the suggestion that sympathies can cross from different places and languages, different peoples of

varied status. She also represents an imagined cultural survival from one era of belief to another: Sibilla exists as a Christian fantasy about a pagan presence from the past, and as such she fulfils a certain function in thinking about forbidden, buried, even secret matters.

'By my voice I shall be known': it is no bad epitaph for a storyteller. (*FBB* 11)

It is the need to find a voice that unites the gossip, the Sibyl, the first narrators of fairy tales, and all those women who have been subject to patriarchal patronage.

Associated with the ancient figure of the Sibyl is the early modern figure of Mother Goose, who inhabits a similar tension. On the one hand she is absurd: redolent of the farmyard, she is earthily and grotesquely comic. On the other hand, she is a fount of wisdom: the tales she tells are not only entertaining but edifying, and carry a considerable weight of what Benjamin calls 'counsel'. It is no coincidence that the earliest literary versions of fairy tales – those of Perrault and his female contemporaries – made sure to adopt the persona of Mother Goose: on the one hand it gave them the credibility of the oral tradition, while on the other it aroused the expectation of pleasure in the reader. Warner speculates that this persona has an impressive pedigree:

The immemorial storyteller, Mother Goose ... is a figure of fun, a foolish, ignorant old woman, a typical purveyor of old wives' tales. But she is also established, by the early eighteenth century, as a Sibyl-Nurse – who instils morality and knowledge of the world, and foresees the future of her charges and prepares them for it. The appended moral, transmitted by the wisdom of old age to the young, was ascribed to this figure, the Sibyl-Nurse, in order to justify the frequent violence, bawdy, and extravagant fantasy of fairytale material. (*FBB* 79)

This may sound a rather cynical account of the act of narration, but the ultimate significance of the figures of Mother Goose and the Sibyl is that they demonstrate the resilience, the adaptability and the subversive power of a voice that has been denied speech, of a gender that has been denied dignity, and of a class that has been denied power.

Though Warner is keen to ensure that we do not overlook the historical context in which the original tellers told their tales, her interest in their continuing potential for challenging orthodoxy prevents her from burdening the book with scholarly detail.

Indeed, she is as deeply interested in what the tales can come to suggest in our time as she is in what was probably intended. Thus, the very terms of the title of her study imply a shift of emphasis: not only is she offering to survey a body of narratives from the perspective of both positive and negative images, both 'blonde' and 'beast', but she is also interested in how our understanding of their relationship has altered. Taking the example of a key story, that of 'Beauty and the Beast', she notes how in the nineteenth century it became subject to an increasingly rarefied interpretation, with the idealized female protagonist (frequently an asexual 'blonde') only being able to love the animalistic antagonist once he had been purged of his 'beastliness'. She is sure this is a travesty of earlier readings of the tale; and, while she is extremely suspicious of the globalized, corporate version of fairy tales currently being foisted on an historically innocent public by the mass media, she finds occasion to compliment the Disney film version (released in 1991). Here 'Beauty' (interestingly, *not* a 'blonde') has to learn to love the 'Beast' as he is, accepting him as a part of nature. For 'the real animal which the Disney Beast most resembles is the American buffalo, and this tightens the Beast's connections to current perceptions of natural good – for the American buffalo, like the grizzly, represents the lost innocence of the plains before man came to plunder'. In short, he 'epitomizes the primordial virtues of the wild' (*FBB* 315).

While Warner has no illusions about multinational entertainment industries, she is alert to the fact that even the most exploitative of commercial enterprises has, at times, to respond to the *Zeitgeist* – in this case, the ecological awareness of a large number of citizens of the United States. For Warner it is necessary, then, to maintain, with her friend Angela Carter, a 'defiant hold on "heroic optimism"', the mood she singled out as characteristic of fairy tales' (*FBB* 197). It is of the very nature of the genre to generate possibilities, for it is, after all, about the triumph of good fortune in the most unlikely circumstances: 'Fairy tales often attack received ideas: monsters turn out to be handsome young princes, beggars princesses, ugly old women powerful and benevolent fairies ...' (*FBB* 415). If we agree with Felix Guattari, quoted by Warner on the last page of her book, that 'figures of power' are open to 'liberatory paths / voices',

71

then we may use fairy tale as a sketch towards 'the possibility of utopia': we can dream of 'transforming this planet – a living hell for over three quarters of its population – into a universe of creative enchantments' (*FBB* 418). Or, as Warner herself concludes:

> The store of fairy tales ... holds out the promise of just those creative enchantments, not only for its own characters caught in its own plotlines; it offers magical metamorphoses to the one who opens the door, who passes on what was found there, and to those who hear what the storyteller brings. The faculty of wonder, like curiosity, can make things happen; it is time for wishful thinking to have its due. (*FBB* 418)

*****

Warner's ambitious novel, *Indigo, or Mapping the Waters* (1992) begins with the telling of a tale. Serafine, the old Caribbean nurse, known affectionately as 'Feeny', is narrating the story of a king who orders the capture of a fat man who has visited his land and is encouraging the young people to hold extravagant parties and to abandon their duties. The king is very possessive about his beautiful young daughter, whom he wants to protect from this outburst of hedonism. But he is also avaricious. So when the fat man's master arrives to offer him a reward for his troubles, he asks that everything he has be made as valuable as gold. His wish is granted, and he is forced to watch not only his material possessions but also his beloved child turn to gold in front of his eyes.

This tale, a variant upon the story of King Midas, is rendered more personal by the narrator's mentioning that during his feasting the fat man talks about having visited a wonderful island. Serafine informs her charge, Miranda, that the island is 'called Enfant-Beauté, Blessed Child' and that it is 'where I was born' (*IMW* 7). But why does the novel begin with Serafine's telling of this tale? Readers are liable to feel unsure at first, even if they infer that she has undergone exploitation; but, by the end of the novel, they will have been offered a thorough exploration of the relation between England and 'Liamuiga'. (That is the original name of the main island – separated by a strait from the subsidiary area of land known as 'Qualie'.) This relationship being traced over a considerable historical span, which includes the rise of European colonialism, the tale might be seen to be Serafine's way of addressing, whether consciously or unconsciously, the theme of colonial greed. For *Indigo* is a novel about the consequences of appropriation, in both the physical and the ideological senses.

This theme is echoed in another tale which 'Feeny' tells, later in the novel, but here she exercises artistic licence to soften her material. Her subject is Manjiku, the terrible male monster who, according to the inhabitants of Liamuiga, devours pregnant women so that he can give birth to their babies. He is hated and feared by all the islanders. Serafine sees it as her duty to sweeten the story for children: she narrates it as a variant on 'Beauty and the Beast', so that Manjiku turns into a handsome young man once he ceases his devouring and shows himself capable of affection. 'For Manjiku was under a curse, you know – (Serafine is talking softly, very softly.) – Only a woman who knew what real loving is could undo its power' (*IMW* 224). We can call this censorship; or we could say that she is exercising the prerogative of all storytellers, to adapt, revise and extend the possibilities of the story she inherits. Perhaps we will find, as we proceed, that the novel itself demonstrates the power of the imagination to help us confront the monstrous events of the past, while maintaining hope for the future.

That said, we must first acknowledge that past. When Europeans chose to settle in their recently discovered 'new world', to dominate, possess and exploit its native inhabitants, they simultaneously undermined the imaginative powers that had sustained those people. As the white settlers fulfilled the destiny which they identified with history – or, more exactly, 'History' with a capital H – they rewrote the myth of those who became subject to them. That would seem to be implicit in the novel's subtitle, which is deliberately ambiguous. 'Mapping the waters' is what the colonial conquerors had to do in order to find their way around the islands they wished to appropriate. But it is also a metaphor for the imposition of western ideas of order on a rich, complex culture which seemed chaotic to the arrogant visitors, convinced of their God-given right to force it into their own model of civilization. For what does the latter really amount to? As Walter Benjamin declared: 'There is no document of civilization which is not at the same time a document of barbarism.' (Benjamin 1, 258) Perhaps with him in mind, Warner may be seen in this novel as attempting 'to brush history against the grain', and resist the triumphal narrative of the West (Benjamin 1, 259).

To understand how she does this, readers need to get their bearings – which is not the easiest task, given the complex plotting. However, the author helpfully provides a list of characters and a map at the beginning of the book, which interested readers should not overlook. The generations of characters are apt to appear confusing as one begins to read, so one must be prepared to do some flicking back and forth to check the *dramatis personae*. Similarly, the geography of 'Enfant-Beauté' needs visualizing as clearly as possible, if one is to negotiate a tortuous sequence of events – including its settlement by both English and French colonialists. But persistence pays off, and after the book is closed, many names and places linger in the imagination. More importantly, one has come to appreciate, even more than in Warner's previous novels, the subtle interweaving of fiction and fact, myth and history, fantasy and realism.

The characters are listed as existing either 'then' (the early seventeenth century, when the island was conquered) or 'now' (the 1940s through to the mid-1980s). Christopher Everard ('Kit') was the pioneer and adventurer who led the English expedition to Limuiga. He subdued the natives by capturing Sycorax, their wise woman, and her adopted daughter Ariel. Antony Everard ('Ant') is his twentieth-century descendant: an old-fashioned patriarch, and something of a hero at sports. His first wife, Estelle Desjours, who was Creole in origin, gives birth to their child, Kit, named after his illustrious ancestor. However, she subsequently dies in a drowning accident – thus prefiguring a later event, as we shall see. Kit, unlike his ancestor, grows up idle and aimless; he marries a girl named Astrid, who turns out to be an alcoholic. They produce a child named Miranda. Ant, meanwhile, becomes the father of Xanthe, after a late second marriage: so, though she is the younger of the two girls, Xanthe is actually Miranda's aunt. In the realm of the 'now', the focus is the contrast between these two, with the one representing the colonizing side of the family and the other, thanks to her Creole ancestry, identification with the colonized.

The mention of one or two of those names will indicate that *Indigo* is to a large extent a creative retelling of Shakespeare's late romance *The Tempest*. Warner herself has remarked that, under the influence of her Catholic upbringing, she chose in writing the novel to adopt a principle familiar to those engaged in the interpretation of the Christian Bible: 'the New Covenant (the present day) fulfils the enigmatic prophecies of the Old (the past) in a typological pattern' (RP 33). 'Typology', then, would read the second testament, the story of Jesus Christ, as the realization of the images, events and characters in the first testament which prefigure his coming: for example, just as Isaac carries the wood for his own sacrifice, so does Jesus carry his own cross; just as Moses and the Hebrews spend forty years in the wilderness, so does Jesus spend forty days. Thus, we might read Warner's novel as the postcolonial fulfilment of the 'enigmatic prophecies' of an ostensibly colonial play by Shakespeare. It is a powerful way of thinking about the way texts exist in time, just as 'typology' itself allows us to see biblical myth as deeply historical (Coupe, 106ff).

It is also worth reflecting that *The Tempest* may be regarded as a dramatic version of a wonder tale, of the sort theorized by Warner in *From the Beast to the Blonde*. Thus, we need to think of the novel as self-reflexive, in that it leaves us in no doubt about its literary source, in that it invites us to compare and contrast Shakespeare's imaginary world with its own, and in that it constantly foregrounds the act of narration. As Serafine tells her first tale (see above), we are informed that 'in her stories everything risked changing shape' (*IMW* 4). Fiction is metamorphosis, tales involve transformation; and a novel that draws attention to these matters is sometimes called 'metafiction'. Thus, it is important to register such moments as that in which Serafine herself declares, of the beautiful princess whose father is so possessive of her: 'Her mother is dead, yes, just like in one of those fairy tales' (*IMW* 6).

As to the specific connection with *The Tempest*, we may recall that Shakespeare's heroine is herself motherless, existing as she does in a fairy-tale setting with a possessive father on a magic island. But where Prospero's magic is an art that enables him to transcend nature and to appropriate the island, in an act suggestive of imperialism, the dominant figure in *Indigo* is

75

Sycorax, the inhabitant whom Prospero subdues. In a sense, the novel is about her power, her skill, her legacy – which, it is implied, no amount of colonial oppression can exorcise. Moreover, its plot is that of *The Tempest* retold from the perspective of the daughter, Miranda, rather than from the father, Prospero. These two aspects – the power of Sycorax and the centrality of Miranda – are complementary, since if the one challenges imperialism and the other challenges patriarchy, the novel demonstrates the intimate connection between those forces.

It is important to recognize, however, that Sycorax is not a native: rather, she can lay claim to having been the first settler on the island, arriving from 'Argier' (Algiers). Warner is not setting out to offer a simple contrast between settled inhabitants and expansionist invaders: her sense of history is too subtle for that. What we are to understand, though, is that Sycorax has a profound empathy with the habitat of the island itself, which is demonstrated in the very skill which gives the novel its title. Warner describes this in prose which itself shows a deep respect for the interaction of nature (environment) and culture (craft). Sycorax is described in earthy, exact terms: 'For the making of indigo, Sycorax needed plenty of sweet water; the steeping of the light foliage gathered from the bushes, the seethings and distillations that followed needed an accessible and constant supply' (*IMW* 90). Warner renders Shakespeare's deliberately vague account of the 'blue-eyed hag' suddenly distinct: 'Over a decade of dyeing, the indigo stained Sycorax blue ... It was easy to mistake her grey eyes for blue as well, for the whites were the colour of the noonday sky, especially when she twisted to look up from a cistern where she was busy steeping the new cloth, turning it, wringing it, rinsing it, to check on the gathering of the storm-clouds and possible rain' (*IMW* 90–1).

But again, we are not to assume that the human being and her landscape can be unthinkingly identified. Sycorax is someone who has made herself at home on the island through skill and strategy, which are worthy of respect. So also Ariel, her adopted daughter, is an Arawak, that is to say a North American tribesperson, who had been brought by European settlers from the Surinam mainland, and who has had to learn the ways of Liamuiga. And to complete the trio we have Dule (later known as Caliban), who arrived on the island when his mother, an

African slave journeying in a slave ship, was thrown overboard off the island's coastline along with many of her companions: Sycorax rescued the child from his mother's womb. Dule, then, is another outsider; but unlike Sycorax and Ariel, he feels misplaced from the start. He longs to return to Africa, from which ideal state he feels himself to have fallen. In his imagination he is continually constructing a 'symbolic ladder' that would take him out of the present and back to his origins: 'Between the time now and the time I can't remember' (*IMW* 96). That said, he shares their intuitive appreciation of Liamuiga's natural beauty and biodiversity.

We can say, then, that these three embody an important sense of identity, that is shattered with the arrival of Kit Everard, leader of the expedition to conquer and settle on Liamuiga. Thus, we may detect a parallel between Shakespeare's and Warner's basic storyline, with Everard taking on the role of Prospero. The difference, of course, lies in the respective authorial assumptions about the ethics of subordination. *Indigo* is an interrogation of western arrogance, and a celebration of the wisdom that it ignores and displaces. In the language of the play, we learn: 'The isle is full of noises, so they say, and Sycorax is the source of many' (*IMW* 77). Then, when strange, hostile noises begin to be heard, we empathize with Sycorax, as she becomes uneasy. And it is the arrival of Dule, born out of callousness and catastrophe, that alerts her to the threat of the future: 'To Sycorax it feels as if she began to die the day the corpses landed on Liamuiga' (*IMW* 77). This is the reality underlying the 'brave new world' that Shakespeare's Miranda thought she had glimpsed when she saw the visitors to her island. The ironies abound: watching the play itself, we know that they are intruders from the 'old world'; reading this novel, we are encouraged to reflect on the consequences of the settling of one 'world' by another.

Sycorax's forebodings are realized. Everard captures both her and Ariel, holding them hostage to secure his safety. He has intercourse with Ariel, who bears a child, Roukoube ('Red Bear Cub'). The transgressive nature of the act means that Sycorax must curse the infant, its product. Though she secures the escape of both Ariel and child from the stockade at the cost of her own life, her curse continues beyond her death. Sycorax dies of the crippling wounds she received when the invaders initially burnt her out of her tree house. In effect, she sinks back into the earth which has been the source of her inspiration for so long. She is buried upright beneath the saman tree in which she had her house: she and the tree become objects of a mystical cult. She is the link between the seventeenth and twentieth centuries, because her 'long death' is imagined as continuing unabated and uncompleted. Her spirit is constantly felt throughout the novel, attempting to arrest the unfolding of history, insofar as it destroys the source of her magic.

But it is Dule who decides to take practical action against the encroachment of imperialism. Defiant about his African roots and his colour, he refuses to capitulate to Everard and his fellow-colonialists. Thus, he instinctively defends Liamuiga. Indeed, for him Manjiku the monster is manifest in the violent invasion of the English (*IMW* 154–5). Not content with his 'symbolic ladder' as a means of asserting his noble identity, he leads a revolt. He tells Ariel of the impending uprising; but she, by contrast, being uneasy about her identity, is unsure how to act. With a vague plan to kill Kit, she inadvertently gives him warning of the impending revolt. Joining it too late, she allows herself and Dule to be captured. Everard and his men punish the latter by splitting his hamstrings so that he can only hobble; they mockingly rename him Caliban. *The Tempest* is continuing to be retold.

The first half of the novel moves rapidly between 'then' and 'now'. The second half of the novel is based almost entirely in the twentieth century, though with the voice of Sycorax continuing to be heard, lamenting the sequence of disasters that she saw beginning in the seventeenth century. In a language ironically reminiscent of Prospero's abandonment of his 'rough magic', she declares that, if only the island could go back to 'those days before everything changed', then 'I would abjure my art then and there, leave off cursing, leave off binding fast and loose with spells' (*IMW* 212). But the author tells us that 'she cannot set limits on her powers, then nor now. Only the faithful who pray to her and draw on her strength can do that' (*IMW* 212–13). Thus, the very nature of belief is at stake: the novel documents its apparent decline, in an age when European reason claims to have triumphed, but demonstrates its residual power.

One of the main events recounted in this part of the novel is the repetition by the modern, global market of the appropriation of the island made earlier by Kit Everard, the colonial adventurer. His descendant inherits both his name and the consequences of that time. We are told that the twentieth-century Kit has himself 'a touch of the tarbrush', his mother being a native of Liamuiga: he is known back home as 'Nigger' Everard. But when he visits the island for the anniversary of its settlement, he feels estranged: he becomes a living embodiment of the displacement that Sycorax heard in the wind. He is naturally if ineffectually protective of Miranda, who herself feels ill at ease in England and is seeking a place where she can find identity and fulfilment. Her concern is not shared by Xanthe, who sets out early on to make her way in the world as it is. As a young woman, she adopts the nickname 'Goldie', indicating her interest in making capital and echoing the story told by Serafine to Miranda. She plans to marry Sy Nebris, a smooth entrepreneur who works in the hotel and catering business. His plan is to 'map out' the waters of the Caribbean, imposing a global culture. The episode of colonialism is repeated, though this time the key factors are not sugar and slavery, but image and tourism.

Kit, being malleable, agrees to help 'sell' the island, given his inwardness with its ways, even though he regrets the way that Xanthe collaborates in Sy's commercial 'package' with a complete disregard for the needs of the islanders. She is totally insensitive to the oppression of native employees by rich customers, and is indifferent to the history of colonialism. However, historical forces do finally impinge on her, and fatally. She is drowned while sailing in a launch to check that Sy and his 'Spice of Life' hotel are safe, after a revolution led by a Muslim fundamentalist, Abdul Malik, who wants to create a radical Islamic state on the island. This, we infer, would have been no more desirable than the act of appropriation which is Sy's tourism industry. As with the colonial past, the point is that the island, and in particular Sycorax's magic, eludes definition. But we are also to infer that even this must have its day. In a parallel with Prospero's final speech, and echoing Ariel's song from *The Tempest*, the drowning is the occasion of a kind of farewell. Firstly it is Xanthe's: 'Sea-changes never come to stillness for some among the dead ... But for Xanthe Everard this was the final transformation: a pearl of rare size and beauty, she had become incapable of further motion in mind or body ...'. Secondly it is Sycorax's: with the recent events in mind, both the imposition of global culture and its Islamic resistance, she foresees a time in the near future when 'the noises of the isle will be still and I – I shall at last come to silence' (*IMW* 376).

As for Miranda, she is seen, by contrast with her half-sister, to go through paroxysms of self-doubt in her attempt to distance herself from Sy's revised form of exploitation. Working as a journalist, she feels guilty when she is sent to do an interview with the avant-garde director of a porno-political film and is castigated by the black actor George Felix for her stance, in denial of her Creole inheritance, of white liberal condescension. Later, however, they meet again, when she is designing tee-shirts for a charity, which he (now called by his Zulu name, Shuka) is to model, and a mutual interest is nurtured. Later still, after several years, she is surprised to find him acting in a Shakespeare play: he is playing Caliban in a performance of *The Tempest*. They fall in love. It is tempting to see this union and its product as signs of a resolution of the residual conflicts of the past, as if the burden of colonialism could be wished away by the neat closure of marriage. But Miranda feels she knows better: she 'wasn't living inside one of Shakespeare's sweet-tempered comedies', she tells herself; she had to accept 'the postmodern condition' (*IMW* 391, 392). But if postmodernity (the historical phase, the era of late capitalism) is about the imposition of shallow, global values on diverse cultures, postmodernism (the cultural negotiation of that phase) is ideally about the creation of novels such as this, in which the very form encourages us to envisage new possibilities of identity. Thus, when finally we learn that Miranda has conceived a child by him, we learn also that the name she gives her is Serafine. Not only has the female hero of *The Tempest* married Caliban. Not only has 'Beauty' married a man who represents centuries of misunderstanding and abuse – in short, her 'Beast'. But also a new kind of living is made possible, a new way of 'mapping the waters'. It is not a matter of 'learning to forget', however. Rather, they have to accept each other, themselves, and the history that has made them what they are. Only by facing and understanding the past can they create the future. 'They had begun play,' we are told, but by 'play' is also meant 'work': 'crossing the lines, crossing the squares, far out on board in the other's sea' (*IMW* 395).

Thus, Serafine, the much-lamented nanny who beguiled the two girls with tales, lives on in memory, just as the wisdom of Sycorax, though she be silent, awaits rediscovery. But what is represented by the infant Serafine – the truly 'blessed child', perhaps – is the possibility of a magic that is not dependent upon the return to Sycorax's time: rather, it is to be found and celebrated now within the human imagination. In this respect, old Serafine, in her capacity as teller of tales, is the emblematic figure. Tales involve transformation, as we have said; magic, then, is present in the power of the story to effect metamorphosis. That is why Warner's novel moves between fantasy and realism, between myth and history: she is enacting a new way of seeing in her own telling of the tale. This new way of seeing is represented by old 'Feeny', a figure reminiscent, in her ability to see beyond the present, with its burden of the past, of the Sibyl. Less grandly, she is a Mother Goose figure. Either way, she speaks for the dispossessed, reminding us of the capacity to envisage a world beyond the given order. Thus, her function in the novel may remind us of the closing statement of *From the Beast to the Blonde*: 'It is time for wishful thinking to have its due'.

We might put this principle another way by saying that the novel demonstrates the dialectic of myth and history. Far from idealizing Sycorax's world, it situates it in order that we may see beyond it. Of her and her followers we are told that 'as yet, they did not know time as a straight line that can be interrupted, even broken, as the people did who were arriving in their archipelago ... they did not possess a past, for they did not see themselves poised on a journey towards triumph, perhaps, or extinction'. In short, they inhabited 'the continuous present tense of existence' (*IMW* 121–2). It is that other view of time, as remorseless, linear progress, that the western invaders bring with them. Thus, we might expect the novel to set up a rigid opposition between them, identifying the one with myth and the other with history, celebrating the one and denigrating the latter. But if we read carefully, we will see that such a contrast is constantly queried.

After all, the colonialists' faith in history as divine destiny is itself mythic. Moreover, both myths, 'primitive' and modern, are predicated on the notion of having fallen. According to the theorist of myth, Mircea Eliade, the main myth of the kind of culture we call (in our arrogance) 'primitive' will be one which assumes an initial harmony from which the community feels itself to have lapsed, and which it tries to regain. In this sense, it does look backwards, towards a moment of origin; but in the modern sense it does not possess an historical past, for it repudiates the idea of temporal sequence. Everything hinges on what can be recovered from the moment of origin in the present. Narrating the myth holds out the possibility of a recovery of 'sacred time' (the moment of creation) and a transcendence of 'profane time' (the experience of the fallen world). Eliade calls this 'the myth of the eternal return'. The present becomes, by virtue of recitation, ritual and remembrance, the 'sacred time' itself. Supposedly more sophisticated myths, such as that of Christianity, may seem to contradict this urge, being about the possibility of redemption at the end of history, as in the story of the apocalypse. But Eliade suggests that this implies the same urge towards 'sacred time' and the same desire to transcend 'profane time', even if the former is pictured as lying ahead of us rather than behind us (Eliade, 68ff).

In *Indigo,* the two kinds of myth are represented by Sycorax and Everard respectively. The painstaking chronology of the novel makes clear that, though the islanders do not know history, and so cannot envisage a line running from past to future, and though their 'continuous present tense' means that they enjoy proximity to the divine, they are nonetheless fallen beings. The difference between them and the Christian colonialists is that the latter have an official theology of 'the fall', derived from the first book of their Bible, and so the concept of a 'paradise lost', with the accompanying concept of a 'paradise regained', is especially acute. 'Paradise' is the very word used by the English invaders to describe Liamuiga, even though Everard laments that 'There'll never be such a place without people in it already' (*IMW* 179–80). Nostalgia for Eden is part of their myth. But so also is the conviction that one has the right to occupy it, disrupt its way of life and oppress its inhabitants. So we need, Warner implies, a mythic way of thinking that goes beyond this impasse. 'Eternal return' is not possible – nor is it desirable, given that the very notion of a paradise is being marketed in our own day by the likes of Sy Nebris, who declares of Liamuiga: 'This is the place of lost time if ever there was one. Island tempo, no hurry, nowhere to go, nothing to do' (*IMW* 295). The 'continuous present tense of existence', Sycorax's mythic time, is being sold as solace for those suffering from the consequences of history. So we need to trust in the spirit of transformation that Serafine's storytelling, and by extension the novel itself, enacts. History becomes myth, myth becomes history. What matters is the infinite potential of the human imagination that makes both possible. Times intersect, the 'sacred' with the 'profane'; characters from a Shakespeare play find themselves acting new roles; voices are heard across the generations, their words finding new meanings in different contexts. And it is all down to the power of the word itself, celebrated in the 'play' of this novel. As the philosopher Paul Ricoeur says, 'the spirit of language' is 'not just some decorative excess or effusion of subjectivity, but *the capacity of language to open up new worlds*'. Or again: 'Language in the making celebrates reality in the making' (Ricoeur, 489, 462).

5

Managing Monsters and *Mermaids in the Basement*

It may seem surprising that a writer whose work draws on mythology to such an extent as does Warner's should take so long to offer her own definitive statement on the nature of myth. What she might reply, with some justification, is that her writing from *The Dragon Empress* to *Indigo* is exploratory rather than illustrative: that is, it is a way of discovering the mythic dimension of culture rather than a demonstration of what she already understands myth to be. However, in 1994 Warner was invited to deliver the Reith Lectures on BBC Radio 4, and she took the opportunity to take stock of the current state of mythography. *Managing Monsters: Six Myths of Our Time* (1994) is about the process by which received narratives may acquire new significance through retelling, with the proviso that both versions are open to critical rereading.

In her foreword to the published lectures, Warner acknowledges again her debt to Roland Barthes, and in particular to his volume of essays *Mythologies*, first published in 1957:

> Barthes's fundamental principle is that myths are not eternal verities, but historical compounds, which successfully conceal their own contingency, changes and transitoriness so that the story they tell looks as if it cannot be told otherwise, that things were always like that and always will be. Barthes's study almost amounts to an exposé of myth, as he reveals how it works to conceal political motives and secretly circulate ideology through society. (*MMM* xiii–xiv)

This is a judicious summary of the theorist's achievement; but implicit in it is a critique. For the trouble with Barthes's approach is that, while it is useful for searching out the lies which the powerful tell in order to persuade the powerless that society cannot be changed, it is not much use to the serious mythographer. That is, it still amounts to a sophisticated variant on the assumption that the word 'myth' connotes falsity (as in such everyday sayings as 'Freedom is just a myth'). It is significant that Warner, whose debt to Barthes was most obvious in her very early work, now begins to express doubts about this approach: 'My own view is less pessimistic; I believe the process of understanding and clarification to which Barthes contributed so brilliantly can give rise to newly told stories, can sew and weave and knit different patterns into the social fabric and that this is a continuous enterprise for everyone to take part in' (*MMM* xiv). Thus, we can detect an ambivalence on Warner's part, far deeper than that which was evident in her invocation of Barthes in *Alone of All Her Sex*. Intellectually, she fully acknowledges how myth may serve the status quo; but her intuition is that myth may also open up possibilities.

We might restate this ambivalence in terms of the tension between 'idelology' and 'utopia', which Ricoeur sees as constituting that social imagination which we call 'mythology'. For if myths are stories which we tell in the present, they may either bind us to the past or they may seek continuity between past and future. They may either offer a confirmation of the world we know or they may offer a vision of a world to which we may aspire. They may delude us with a false explanation of the way things are or they may facilitate a true exploration of a radical alternative. For Ricoeur, the latter can only take place when we stop reading myths literally, and we start allowing their symbolic dimension full rein. Thus, while it is necessary to subject the ideological aspect of myth to critical scrutiny, it is important not to stop there. We must go forward to discover the 'post-critical' potential of myth:

> In other words, it is because the survival of myth calls for perpetual historical reinterpretation that it involves a critical component. Myths are not unchanging and unchanged antiques which are simply delivered out of the past in some naked, original state. Their specific identity depends on the way in which each generation receives or interprets them according to their needs, conventions, and ideological motivations. Hence the necessity of critical discrimination between liberating and destructive modes of reinterpretation. (Ricoeur, 486)

So the world of myth is only accessible by way of attention to the word. We need to respond to what he calls 'the spirit of language', which for Ricoeur is evident not only in myth but in any highly imaginative writing (what he here calls 'poetry'):

> By the [phrase] spirit of language we intend not just some decorative excess or effusion of subjectivity, but *the capacity of language to open up new worlds*. Poetry and myth are not just nostalgia for some forgotten world. They constitute a disclosure of unprecedented worlds, an opening on to other *possible* worlds which transcend the limits of our *actual* world. (Ricoeur, 489–90)

In the light of the above, it would be a fair conjecture that Warner's own understanding of myth is ultimately utopian rather than ideological; in short, that she belongs with Ricoeur rather than Barthes. Here is her definition, made in the course of the first of the Reith Lectures:

> A myth is a kind of story told in public, which people tell one another; they [i.e., myths] wear an air of ancient wisdom, but that is part of their seductive charm. Not all antiques are better than a modern design – especially if they're needed in ordinary, daily use. But myth's own secret cunning means that it pretends to present the matter as it is and always must be; at its heart lies the principle, in the famous formula of Roland Barthes, that history is turned into nature. But, contrary to this understanding, myths aren't writ in stone, they're not fixed ... Myths offer a lens which can be used to see human identity in its social and cultural context – they can lock us up in stock reactions, bigotry and fear, but they're not immutable, and by unpicking them, the stories can lead to others. Myths convey values and expectations which are always evolving, in the process of being formed, but – and this is fortunate – never set so hard they cannot be changed again, and newly told stories can be more helpful than repeating old ones. (*MMM* 13–14)

Thus, her project in *Managing Monsters* is to encourage the 'newly told stories' to be genuinely liberating, so that mythology becomes part of a process of creative emancipation: 'By holding up to the light modern mythical nodes of this kind I hope to loosen, in some cases, their binding grip on the imagination. Replying to one story with another which unravels the former has become central to contemporary thought and art – text as well as image' (*MMM* 4).

86

That, on reflection, was exactly what Warner was about in *Indigo*, with its radical revision of *The Tempest*. So it is worth noting that in the fifth of her Reith Lectures, 'Cannibal Tales: The Hunger for Conquest', she documents narratives arising from colonization which presented the colonized as monstrous, engaged in barbaric practices. Her point is that the myth of the cannibal tells us more about its tellers than about the 'other' which they misrepresent: 'Cannibalism is used to define the alien but actually mirrors the speaker. By tarring the savage with the horror of cannibalism, settlers, explorers, colonisers could vindicate their own violence – it's a psychological manoeuvre of great effectiveness. Seeing the conquered as brute barbarians helped the confidence of the first empire builders' (*MMM* 74). In *The Tempest*, the name 'Caliban' is clearly reminiscent of 'cannibal'. But Warner refuses to dismiss the drama as simply colonial ideology: she points out that it is made clear how welcoming Caliban was to Prospero and Miranda on their arrival on the island, even though he is described derisively as 'savage', as a 'freckled whelp, hag-born'. The legacy of Shakespeare's play, like all great art, offers later readers the chance of reinterpretation, so that rather than reading it as unambiguously oppressive, they may discover in it a new, liberating significance: 'This contradiction at the heart of the characterisation has turned Caliban into a mythic figure beyond the confines of *The Tempest* itself, and he has consequently become a key symbol in the discussion of colonialism, and its attendant ills, including racism' (*MMM* 75). And Warner might have added that he has been central to the postcolonial imagination, as evinced by her own novel *Indigo*.

However, it is hard to believe that some contemporary artistic representations of monstrosity will ever be open to the redemptive gesture of reinterpretation. In her first lecture, 'Monstrous Mothers: Women Over the Top', Warner takes the example of the film *Jurassic Park*, in which the velociraptors wreak havoc, having found a way to breed despite the safeguards put in place by scientists: 'Thus female organisms, in the film, prove ultimately uncontrollably fertile, resistant to all the constraints of the men of power. The story can be reduced to a naked confrontation between nature coded female with culture coded male: the bristling, towering, jagged, megavolt fence cannot hold the primeval at a stage of intelligent evolution' (*MMM* 2). But the significance of *Jurassic Park* is wider still, and reflects the ideology of our media-dominated age: 'One of the stories in mass circulation today is a very old one, but it's taken on a new vigour: women in general are out of control, and feminism in particular is to blame' (*MMM* 3). She explains:

> Feminism today has become a bogey, a whipping boy, routinely produced to explain all social ills: women's struggle for equality of choice in matters of sex, their grasp of sovereignty over their bodies, are blamed in particular for the rise in family breakdown, the increase of divorce, and the apparently spiralling delinquency and violence of children. ... Men are no longer in control, mothers are not what they used to be, and it's the fault of Germaine Greer, *Cosmopolitan* and headlined stars who choose to be single mothers, like Michelle Pfeiffer. (*MMM* 3–4)

Here the 'myth' stands in close proximity to the 'ideology'; the dimension of 'utopia' is distant indeed.

If the present function of myth can obscure the future, it often does so by obscuring the past – from which, after all, it derives. An historical sense is required in order to appreciate the hidden residue of accumulated meaning. There are, after all, as she has implied, ancient examples of demonic females. She specifically mentions the myth of Medea: 'Among bad mothers of fantasy she is the worst ...'. But, in accordance with her historicizing sense, she documents the shift within antiquity from a more generalized, benign picture of Medea to the more specific, sinister one associated with the play written by one of the Athenian tragedians, which then took hold of the social imagination: 'Euripides's tragedy, written in the fifth century BC, introduced Medea the child-killer, and has made this side of her much more familiar than other texts, which stress her enchantments and in some cases her humanity. We pick and choose bad mothers to suit our times just as we pick our dinosaurs' (*MMM* 7). Here the only response is critical scrutiny: we need to have our scholarly wits about us if we are to counter the dominance of such versions of famous myths. More generally, we need to interrogate the very nature of monstrosity, and its link with mythology.

This Warner does in her second lecture, 'Boys Will Be Boys: The Making of the Male'. She notes the alarming popularity of computer games which afford adolescent males the opportunity to obliterate a demonic enemy. On the one hand, the idea of these games, that the hero slays monsters, is not that different from Greek myths such as those of Jason or Hercules. On the other hand, what is different is that now the slaughter is the sole purpose of the plot. Destruction is the chief focus. Warner reflects:

> Myths and monsters have been interspliced since the earliest extant poetry from Sumer: the one often features the other. The word 'myth', from the Greek, means a form of speech, while the word 'monster' is derived, in the opinion of one Latin grammarian, from *monestrum*, via *moneo*, and encloses the notions of advising, of reminding, above all of warning. But *moneo*, in the word *monstrum* has come under the influence of the Latin *monstrare*, to show, and the combination neatly characterises the form of speech myth often takes: a myth shows something, it's a story spoken to a purpose, it issues a warning, it gives an account which advises and tells often by bringing into play showings of fantastical shape and invention – monsters. Myths define enemies and aliens, and in conjuring them up they say who we are and what we want, they tell stories to impose structure and order. Like fiction, they can tell the truth even while they're making it all up. (*MMM* 19)

Here is where knowledge of the past is necessary if we are to confront the present and prepare for the future. Without memory of what mythology has involved, we are in no position to offer a critique of its current reduction, and so lay the foundations for new, richer retellings. For, if the myths of today's mass culture are focused entirely on killing the 'other', then we have to heed the warnings about the nature of the self which wants to do the killing: 'The acute, painful problem is that these manufactured monsters are ourselves; and ourselves especially as the male of the species' (*MMM* 22). And how do we assess the impoverishment of mythology involved? We need to reconsider our mythic legacy. For, as Warner insists: 'Stories held in common make and remake the world we inhabit' (*MMM* 93).

Thus, she considers the complexity of a figure like Odysseus, as he features in Homer's epic. While this great hero is capable of violence, that is by no means the extent of his powers. Rather, we celebrate him as 'the hero who lives by his wits': he is the trickster rather than the tough man:

In Homer, Odysseus tells the Cyclops that his name is Nobody. So, when Odysseus blinds the Cyclops in his one eye, the giant howls for help to his father the god of the sea and the other Olympians. But all the gods hear is his cry, 'Nobody has blinded me.' And so they do nothing.

This trick from the *Odyssey* is literally one of the oldest in the book. But a gleeful use of cunning and high spirits against brute force, a reliance on subterfuge have almost faded from heroic myth today. In the prevailing popular concept of masculinity, as reflected in comics, rock bands, street fashion, Clint Eastwood or Arnold Schwarzenegger movies, the little man, the riddler or trickster, has yielded before the type of warrior hero, the paradigm of the fittest survivor. (*MMM* 25)

If we could regain this paradigm of heroism, and see through the cult of violent assertion which dominates our age, we could begin to tell ourselves tales that open up possibilities rather than confine us to our sterile 'social Darwinism' (a crude reduction of Darwin's subtle hypothesis about evolution, applied to human interaction).

Ancient myths, modern retellings: so far so good. But we also need to be able to recognize distinctively modern myths when they arise. The mythographer must be especially alert to 'mythopoeia', the power of making as well as remaking myth. According to Warner, a good example of this is Mary Shelley's famous novel of 1818. Shrewdly responding to the cult of scientific rationalism, she knew that reason can 'beget monsters', in Goya's famous phrase. However, the book is much more than a satire on the fanaticism of scientists. It is, we are told, a radical enquiry into the need for love: '*Frankenstein* has become *the* contemporary parable of perverted science, but this reading overlooks the author's much more urgent message. Mary Shelley grasped the likelihood that a man might make a monster in his own image and then prove incapable of taking responsibility'. Victor Frankenstein 'rejects and wants to destroy the being he's generated from his own intelligence and imagination; he can only flee, and then, when confronted, offer mortal combat – in the desire to be the victor, as his name suggests' (*MMM* 20).

Hence Shelley's myth is a radical interrogation into the nature of monstrosity, in the course of which it offers a prophecy of our cultural malaise: 'The book *Frankenstein* offers a double allegory of monsters' double presence: at one level they're emanations of ourselves, but at another, they're perceived as alien, abominable and separate so that we can deny them, and zap them into oblivion at the touch of a button' (*MMM* 21). Unlike contemporary computer games and horror films, the novel encourages us to sympathize with the creature's plea to be given a mate, his desperate desire for affection:

> Current tales of conflict and extermination never hear the monster say: 'I am malicious, because I am miserable.' Or: 'Make me happy, and I shall again be virtuous.' The phrases sound absurd, because we're so accustomed to expect the hero to have no other way of managing the monsters than slaying them. (*MMM* 22)

Our failure to understand or appreciate the modern myth of Frankenstein's monster means that we are trapped in a vicious circle of violence. Mary Shelley's kind of imagination is urgently required because it provides sustenance for a critique of the ideological aspect of our current mythology: it shows us how our dominant narratives keep us where we are. Thus, Warner ends her account of the visionary novelist with the following eulogy:

> In Mary Shelley's later, apocalyptic novel, significantly called *The Last Man*, the hero exclaims, 'This, I thought, is Power! Not to be strong of limb, hard of heart, ferocious and daring; but kind, compassionate and soft.'
>
> It's a measure of the depths of our present failure of nerve that these words sound ridiculous, embarrassing, inappropriate, that Verney's cry strikes one as a heap of hooey – a foolish dream, a chimaera. Mary Shelley's utopianism is too ardent for our cynical times. But we can take away from her work the crucial knowledge that monsters are made, not given. And if monsters are made, not given, they can be unmade, too. (*MMM* 31)

From ideology to utopia is a large leap, but it is not difficult once one has realized – with Ricoeur and, it would seem, Warner too on this evidence – that the social imagination is not a fixed state. Mythology lives by renewal. Dead myths which trap us need critique; and the ultimate critique is a gesture towards a different way of living. Myths that we value carry that promise.

*****

We have used the term 'mythopoeia' to describe Mary Shelley's work, as praised by Warner. But *Frankenstein* is at the same time a reworking of two ancient myths about the creation of humanity: Genesis (the monster being a variant upon Adam); and Prometheus (Frankenstein himself being a demonic version of the Greek hero, who created and nurtured human beings). As such, it is a work of mythography as much as a work of mythopoeia. Then again, appreciation of the author's achievement will probably entail a recognition that the two processes are complementary. Warner is herself a good example of someone who has demonstrated this throughout her writing career. Her fiction and her non-fiction are both equally mythopoeic and mythographic; she retells and she recreates mythology at one and the same time.

Indeed, her first collection of short stories, *The Mermaids in the Basement* (1993), is one of the most sustained exercises in the extension of mythic meaning that exists in contemporary fiction. But to put it that way is to imply that Warner's narrative skills are subordinated to a theoretical agenda. In some cases, this may seem to be the case, but on the whole we are easily able to suspend our disbelief, as we imagine Eve as a young girl of the present day, traumatized by the loss of her virginity ('The First Time'), or as we hear the story of the flood retold with devastating frankness by Noah's daughter-in-law ('Full Fathom Five'). As these two examples indicate, Warner is particularly concerned in this volume with the survival and status of biblical myth. Hence another story, 'Salvage', reworks the myth of the rescue of the infant Moses, representative of an oppressed people, as told in the book of Exodus. Here the baby in the bulrushes rescued and adopted by the Pharaoh's daughter becomes a Vietnamese foundling, rescued and adopted by the English wife of a war correspondent.

Formulaic as one or two of the fictional exercises may seem, the volume as a whole is persuasive as a revival of myth. One story which stands out is yet another reworking of a biblical source. This is 'The Legs of the Queen of Sheba'. We know from the biblical original that King Solomon invited the beautiful female monarch to his court, hoping to establish the superiority of Israel to a neighbouring country. We know too that he was seduced not only by her beauty but also by her power of rhetoric. We may even recall that in *The Lost Father* an operatic version of the narrative is staged in order to justify Mussolini's invasion of Abyssinia. Further researches into Warner's interest in the story will reveal that in 1991 she wrote the libretto for an opera based upon it; again, the Queen of Sheba is related, in *From the Beast to the Blonde*, to the tradition of female storytelling and of survival through narrative guile. What particularly fascinates Warner is the legend surrounding that visit: aware of the rumours that a beautiful face hid a demonic character, and advised that he would detect the latter if her lower limbs were revealed, Solomon arranged for his royal visitor to step over a frozen river, so that he would be able to see from the reflection whether she had the legs of an animal. This legend, which one might read as implicitly associating patriarchal power with contempt for the female, is taken as the basis for a contemporary story of sexual mores.

The modern-day narrator is a female academic attending a conference in Jerusalem. Acting as hostess to an informal drinks party in her hotel room, she is resolved not to fall into the role of pleasing the men by way of flirtation or of emphasizing her own beauty. However, in the course of the conversation, she finds herself going along with their coarse sexual humour; and at one point in the evening, having joined in a discussion about what men find attractive in women, she proudly and provocatively displays her legs. After her colleagues depart, the narrator castigates herself for betraying her own sex, and for confirming the power relationship that exists, even in the liberal academy, between male and female. Yet, at the end of the story, when she visits the hill near the Old City of Jerusalem, where Solomon's harem was supposed to have been lodged, she finds herself wishing to interpret the biblical tale in positive, amorous terms. She wants to believe that there was a genuine love between Solomon and the Queen of Sheba. Moreover, the very atmosphere of the place, with its strong aroma of fruit trees and its breathtaking views, enforces this sentimental impulse, despite her best endeavours to remain true to her feminist ideals. She is under the spell of the famously erotic 'Song of Songs':

> There were sounds, though, and scents; above all, a song. (*Make haste, my beloved, and be thou like to a roe or a young hart upon the mountains of spices.*) I wanted not to hear. Fight back, I said to myself. Resist the longing. Ass's hooves are fine. Hairy legs are fine. Don't let yourself hear the song. And don't listen, when you do. (*MB* 160)

These are the final words of the story. It is a far more effective ending than a defiant affirmation of women's rights would have been. Warner is too subtle a writer to present a simple case against patriarchy; in exploring the fascination of the biblical myth, with its persuasive associations, both erotic and spiritual, she demonstrates the complexity and the continuing relevance of its legacy.

But scripture is not the extent of Warner's sources. In keeping with the preoccupations of *Managing Monsters*, we get a substantial retelling of a Greek hero myth, that of Theseus. In that story, the hero slays the Minotaur in the Cretan labyrinth, by help of the king of Crete's daughter, Ariadne. He escapes with her, only to subsequently abandon her on the island of Naxos, where she receives the amorous attentions of Dionysus. The myth is usually read as a vindication of the wandering warrior, who proves himself by slaying monstrous enemies; but the myth carries with it its own warning, given that Theseus's arrogance – the very arrogance that allows him to desert the woman without whom his exploit would have failed – results in the death of his own father. Theseus forgets to change the sails of his ship from black to white, so preoccupied is he by his own success: seeing the black sails in the distance as he stands waiting on the cliffs, Aegeus believes that his son has perished on his quest, and so fatally flings himself into the sea below. The ancient stories are never as simplistic as is the contemporary cult of violent entertainment, as Warner makes clear in her Reith Lectures. Now, in a story entitled 'Ariadne after Naxos', she explores a further potential dimension of the tale: what the abandoned heroine herself learns from the whole episode.

It is Ariadne herself who narrates, revealing that she and her daughter Chloe have been accepted by the island's exclusively female community. This silent, celibate sisterhood nurtures a spiritual wisdom that thrives by virtue of excluding any male presence from Naxos. The mother and daughter seem content with their lives, but there are hints of unease: 'We have difficulty keeping this paradise in order: the earth outruns our effort at husbandry' (*MB* 98). Again: 'So much fruitfulness: like a wave, its greatest expansion is also its breaking point, when the fruit will lose the shape that gives its identity, its integrity' (*MB* 98–9). Ariadne secretly knows that, while she would never allow herself to be betrayed by a man like Theseus again, she cannot live the rest of her life in terms of denial and exclusion. She must acknowledge the fullness of earthly existence.

Thus, when the Minotaur reappears – not slain, but spayed – she knows she must come to terms with him. His very existence demands a response: 'He let out a hoarse whinny and, fixing us with his sharp, caper-like eyes fringed with white lashes, he butted me on the thigh with his dark, cracked hoof, and threw his great head back in the air' (*MB* 108). However, she cannot remain tied to her brother, defining herself against him. She has first to accept him again as her own flesh and blood, then go beyond what he has come to mean to her. When a male figure identified only as 'you' arrives on the island, Ariadne gradually falls in love with him and decides that it is time to move on. In doing so, she will finally come to terms with the figure conquered by her previous lover. She can see him for what he is because she can see him for what he has been: 'It was my Minotaur's constant, bulky shadow I'd lost: my companion in rancour, the foil to my wallowing self-abasement. I'd shed him, my other self, my monster of loathing' (*MB* 118). It is as if Ariadne has come to understand the meaning of the myth she has inhabited, as she narrates it all again from a new perspective. As a female, she does not have to define herself as subservient to the hero or as defined against the apparent villain. Mythic meaning is richer than that: 'I can't make my life fit any one gospel; I'm an apostate to the community I shared for a time' (*MB* 119). For she has realized that 'fruitfulness of the soul grows in contingency' (*MB* 120); and so she is much more 'fruitful' in this new life, contingent upon 'you', but neither subservient nor defined.

Warner, then, has shown herself capable of finding the hidden potential within apparently oppressive stories, so that their female protagonists may find new life, discovering 'fruitfulness of the soul' and overcoming the most hostile of circumstances. Repressed, buried voices begin to speak in this volume, thanks to the author's willingness to engage with the rich complexity of the tradition. The clue is in the epigraph from Emily Dickinson which gives Warner her title: 'I started Early – Took my Dog – / And visited the Sea / The Mermaids in the Basement / Came out to look at me...' (*MB* v).

6

No Go the Bogeyman and *The Leto Bundle*

From the Beast to the Blonde concentrated on female experience, explaining the function of characters by reference to the anxieties of the female teller of the fairy tale. *Managing Monsters* surveyed representations of both male and female demons, arguing that they equally reflect the ambivalence of contemporary culture. Warner's next non-fictional work is an ambitious volume that seems designed to comprehend and go beyond both those previous works. *No Go the Bogeyman: Scaring, Lulling and Making Mock* (1998), ostensibly a history of the male demon, manages to explore more or less every conceivable aspect of fear, whether evident in song or story, in myth or ritual, in painting or film.

Curiously, however, Warner's ambitiousness of scope seems to sit at odds with her willingness to espouse a thesis that is essentially a confirmation of one particular theorization of fear, namely the psychoanalytic. We have noted how she sought to challenge the Freudian reading of fairy tale by querying its focus on the child and by stressing the domestic context of adult anxiety which lay behind the original narration. She used history to counter the more facile assumptions of psychoanalysis. Here, though, she seems content to elaborate one of the most familiar of Freudian notions, that of projection. Psychoanalysis explains the nature of horror by seeing both individuals and whole communities as projecting their secret fears onto an external figure, which they then demonize. Certainly, this tactic of the psyche makes perfect sense of the 'bogeyman'. But *No Go the Bogeyman* is not meant to be read as a straightforward documentation of this process. We might note, for example, that Warner makes it clear in the introduction that she has in mind at least two other authorities besides Freud on the way the human mind treats terror. One is Aristotle, who distinguished between art and life in terms of representation and experience – between, we might say, the safe and the scary. In particular, he argued that tragic drama was an art that allowed its audience to find pleasure – or, more accurately, relief – in witnessing extreme and disturbing events on stage. Thus, Warner does not need to rely on Freud's model of projection when she has the Aristotelian model of catharsis, which comprehends it. That model sees projection being subsumed by purgation: art is the psyche's best means of transcending the fear which it creates. Another authority invoked is Edmund Burke, the mid-eighteenth century exponent of the principle of the 'sublime': pain becomes pleasurable when it is apprehended in aesthetic form; we enjoy having our all-too-familiar world threatened momentarily by images of extremity, disturbance and death (*NGB* 6, 9). Thus, while Warner is working in closer proximity to psychoanalytic theory than previously, it would be a mistake to read *Bogeyman* as a simply Freudian argument.

For, beyond the choice of theoretical perspectives, it is myth which is the focus. One particular myth provides Warner with her best example of how the imagination gives form to fear, allowing it to be both undergone and overcome. She begins her book by dwelling on the significance of the infancy narrative of a famous Greek hero: 'The story of Dionysus, torn to pieces by the Titans as a baby, itself represents the power of art to overcome that lurking fear within – specifically, that the bogeyman in the dark wants to gobble us up' (*NGB* 9). The very idea of those monstrous creatures attacking a defenceless child sends a shiver down the spine; and yet it does more, when told as a tale, for it innoculates us against the very fear it provokes. Her reading of this myth sets the agenda for the whole book.

The three terms of Warner's subtitle give us the structure of her argument, which is a three-stage thesis. Firstly, she demonstrates that people have always been disposed to find experience 'scaring'. Horror is human. The 'bogeyman' is a necessary invention, symbolizing as he does all those negative forces with which we have to come to terms: pain, death, evil.

Secondly, she explores how it is equally characteristic of our species to find a means to dispel fear of the 'bogeyman' and of all he represents through song, rhyme, chant, lullaby – in short, by the act of 'lulling'. Thirdly, she celebrates the capacity to laugh away the 'bogeyman', to defy demonic power by 'making mock' of it. For if horror is human, so too is the humour that might overcome it.

Part One, 'Scaring', opens with a fuller account of the identity of the bogeyman. As if to pay her dues to psychoanalysis, Warner discusses, in this initial overview, the fascination of the figure of the 'sandman'. Those who know Freud's essay on 'The Uncanny' will recall that it centres on a reading of a short story by E. T. A. Hoffmann, in which a young man is driven to madness and finally suicide by this demonic phenomenon (Freud, 335–76). The allusion to this account of the 'sandman' is sufficient to remind us that he was not always the benign presence that is suggested by children's folklore of recent years. He was originally an ogre, not a figure analogous to Wee Willie Winkie, as he more frequently appears nowadays. Warner briefly reminds us of Freud's fascination with him, but only as a preamble to a celebration of David Lynch's film *Blue Velvet*, in which Roy Orbison's song 'In Dreams' is given a sinister turn by association with the intrusive presence in a sleepy, conventional North American town of the unhinged character played unforgettably by Dennis Hopper *(NGB* 32). It is artists such as Lynch rather than theorists such as Freud, it is implied, who have done most to help us negotiate the dark side of the sandman. It is, though, thanks to psychoanalysis that we are able to recognize the return of the repressed so readily. Warner is working in a field which psychoanalysis opened up.

That said, she is always ready to challenge the authority of Freud himself. Thus, in the next chapter, 'My Father He Ate Me Up', she addresses that all too influential hypothesis, the Oedipus complex. The original myth concerns a son who is abandoned at birth because the oracle has warned that he will grow up to kill his own father and marry his own mother. This he does anyway, albeit unwittingly. Freud interpreted the myth in terms of the 'family romance', and generalized from it that all male children go through a phase of hostility to the father and desire for the mother. Warner pertinently reminds us that the interest of the original myth lies as much in the father's hostility to the child as in the child's hostility towards the father: Freud has chosen to ignore the initial violence of Laius to Oedipus (the king gives orders that the baby be tied down to the earth and left to die). Freud's complex, based tentatively on a highly selective reading of an ancient Greek story, is for her a classic case of nineteenth-century myth-making. (Warner sees Freud as following on from all those thinkers of that century who sought explanations in origins, creatively interpreted. Her attribution of the specific theory to that period is vindicated, we might add, by the fact that *The Interpretation of Dreams*, in which the case of Oedipus is addressed, was published in the last year of the nineteenth century, even though the fact it was dated 1900, in response to a request from Freud, has led many Freudians to see it as issuing in the twentieth-century view of the mind.) She does not condemn this kind of myth-making: given her own interest in the overlap between mythography and mythopoeia, she could hardly do so. But she does warn us that we have to be on our guard, and careful not to attribute scientific certainty to what is a highly imaginative conjecture, resulting from a curious inability, in one who was obsessed by ambivalence, to see both sides of a situation: 'Freud's insistence on the son's murderous intentions towards the father effaces paternal animus – the foundation myth of Abraham and Isaac, of God the Father and Christ, of Oedipus exposed by Laius – in the interests of emphasizing the father's vulnerability' (*NGB* 69). The man who reminded us of the demonic side of the sandman could yet fail to do justice to the figure of father-as-ogre.

But we still await a proper definition of 'ogre'. Warner provides this in a chapter entitled 'The Devil's Banquet'. Here we are reminded of the etymology: 'ogre' comes from the Latin 'Orcus', another name for Hades, the Greek god of the underworld (also known as Pluto in the Roman context). In other words, the ogre belongs in what came to be known in the Christian era as 'hell'. But the geography, characterization and iconography of monstrosity are complex, and need spelling out:

> Male ogres and giants predominantly inhabit the elements of fire and earth: in Greek myth, their natural haunts are underworlds inside mountains, labyrinths, caverns, swamps, bogs, volcanoes – the predecessors of the Christian hell, which is fiery, unlike Hades. Atlas

the Titan is doomed to shoulder the Earth, Polyphemus the Cyclops dwells in a dark cave. Dante, brilliantly combining the classical and Christian schemata of the infernal regions, casts the giants as Satan's own bodyguards, a rampart of towers sunk deep into Cocytus' pit of ice. Giants are not identical with ogres, but they share characteristics, stories and meaning. Looming like towers, the *Inferno's giganti* strike terror in the poet ... (*NGB* 95)

Fear of being dominated by devils is simultaneously fear of having one's own identity denied. The bogeyman threatens to destroy what we are. Hence, as Warner demonstrates, through further reference to Dante but also to folklore and popular symbolism, the figure of the ogre may often be guilty of cannibalism.

At this point, one might expect Warner to refer back to her dramatization of the plight of Caliban, identified by his very name with the monstrous figure of the cannibal; but, on reflection, that would raise other issues, which she has effectively discussed in her Reith Lectures. Her focus here is on the effect that the figure of the devouring ogre has on us. Who can forget the horror of first reading the *Inferno*, with its motif of being eaten eternally? Thus: 'cannibalism of the perpetual variety practised in hell becomes the preferred and potent metaphor for the obliteration of self that is the fate of sinners. The infernal body is forever devouring or being devoured: hell is a devils' banquet and Satan its master of ceremonies, and the damned are trapped in a perpetual cycle of metamorphosis without closure' (*NGB* 102). From Dante and medieval iconography to the contemporary child's nightmares may seem a large leap, but Warner insists it is one we should be prepared to make: 'Hell is frequently configured as a profane restaurant, in which all the guards are vampires and cannibals. The haunters of nurseries, the child-stealers, the bogeys behave indistinguishably from these emissaries of death' (*NGB* 104).

Which leads us to the second part of her book, 'Lulling'. In isolation, this reflection on the nature of a mother's songs to her children might have been rather bland. But in the context of the whole thesis, it assumes crucial significance. Warner sees the lullaby as a kind of magic, deeply ambiguous in the 'charm' it effects. On the one hand, it is designed to put the baby to sleep; on the other, it is designed to ward off danger. Sleep being a traditional prefigurement of death, the unease behind the simple song becomes evident. A similar tension is felt in the very language employed: the words are meant to keep the bogeyman at bay; but of course, in order to dispel the ogre he must first be invoked. So the charm's power is a confined power, strictly limited by the inevitability of pain, disaster, and mortality. 'A lullaby is a weak domestic magic, alert to its own inadequacy' (NGB 194). For example, 'Rock-a-bye baby on the tree top' is about what terrible things might happen, even while it 'lulls' the child into a feeling of warmth and security (NGB 197).

Pursuing the legacy of the lullaby, Warner speculates on the attraction which the song of the nightingale has traditionally held for storytellers and poets. Ovid in the *Metamorphoses* recounted the tale of Philomela, the maiden raped by King Tereus: he cut out her tongue so that she could not report the incident, but she turned into a nightingale and sang out the story for all to hear. Shakespeare alludes to that song in *A Midsummer Night's Dream*, when he has the fairies sing a 'sweet lullaby' to Titania, invoking Philomela by name. Thereafter, the 'lulling' convention incorporated the terrible tale of Philomela, in keeping with its principle that death shadows sleep, just as the threat of disaster always impinges on our sense of peace; death and disaster require to be acknowledged. Warner proceeds, in her neat history of the nightingale's symbolic power in the context of lulling, or wishing to be lulled, to make a subtle distinction between two Romantic poets. Keats's 'Ode to a Nightingale' makes as much as possible of the Ovidian associations: 'the birdsong becomes a "high requiem" and fades from his hearing as a "plaintive anthem".' However: 'John Clare, needled by Keats's antiquarian and mythologizing observation of nature in his ode, observed the nightingale in the wild ... [and] transcribed its melody as spontaneous poetic language'. Here Warner quotes from *The Progress of Ryhme* (sic): 'tweet tweet tweet jug jug'. Having done so, she indicates how the legacy was given a further twist by Eliot's decision to quote Clare in the great modernist poem, *The Waste Land*: for 'Eliot switched the emphasis from Clare's wondrous, blithe, delicate acoustics to Philomel's rape and mutilation' (NGB 227).

Lest this brief literary history be taken as a diletannte's digression, far in excess of her chosen subject in Part Two, namely the nature of 'lulling', Warner uses such material to lead up to a generalization which is strikingly direct and decisive:

> The variations in historical response to the nightingale pose charged questions about the inherent emotive qualities of music, that stout defence against fear. Is the bird's song intrinsically 'plaintive', or do human ears hear its mood through other, extraneous conductors? And is a dirge consoling in itself, however melancholy the melody and the pace? Do requiems and laments steady us, like lullabies? And could it be that this power of music is linked to the nature of language? Are they both systems that order disorder, that have a calming, soothing and hopeful effect on the listener, enabling him to let go of fears and sorrows? This would explain how the same musical sequence – the nightingale's – can strike the human ear as 'out-sobbing songs' or as 'joyous' outpourings. Unlike birdsong, however, human song is a willed representation, attempting to match feeling and sound. Yet human song echoes birdsong in that its effect does not depend on the emotional content of the music; and, oddly, it lifts the spirits, however doleful it sounds. This is the power of artifice, that it can induce feelings different from those it represents. Singing is a charm against the dark: in their whole range of expression, verbal and musical, however peculiar; sad, harsh and bitter, lullabies work. (*NGB* 227–8)

There are large issues being addressed here, far larger than the apparently whimsical title of Warner's book suggests. What we might have taken to be a survey of different ways in which we cope with being frightened has turned out to be an enquiry into the nature of language, of art and of the psyche. Lullabies, which we might otherwise have dismissed as childish diversions, are here celebrated as continuous with the most dignified literary expression. Lulling, which is the kind of art we encounter as babies, is addressing the same conflicts as we find articulated at greater length in other genres, such as elegy and tragedy. The negative side of the psyche demands representation, which it gets from very early on, thanks to the human capacity for artifice: 'sad, harsh and bitter, lullabies work'.

Part Three takes up this aspect of the human approach to fear: 'Making Mock' offers a general history of the status of the demonic realm, and how it has been dealt with. In traditional societies, the fantastic figure of the monster, ogre or devil was

102

perceived as an external force, independent of human imagination. In the modern period, fear and fantasy began to be located internally. The very faith in reason which we call rationalism involved the attempt to overcome an irrational sense of dread whose source was understood to be an error of mental operations. The counter-movement of Romanticism proclaimed that the capacity to find horror within us was an indication of our psychological complexity, and so merited elaborate exploration. Hence the importance of the 'grotesque', by which the enjoyment of strangeness, distortion and derangement became an aspect of literary experience. We may think of the rise of the Gothic novel; also, of the wealth of weird characters created by Dickens. Finally, within postmodernity, the 'grotesque' has become an end in itself; indeed, the whole culture has become a strange, surface phenomenon, with no aim beyond the play of images. We may think of the popularity of 'slasher' videos, where the experience of horror is everything, with plot, characterization, theme and moral purpose being of little importance. Popular culture is pervaded by this kind of estrangement (*NGB* 246ff).

In charting the move from the 'early' to the 'late grotesque', from modernity to postmodernity, Warner takes in all sorts of representation. In identifying the source of the grotesque itself, she looks to Goya's famous sketch, *The Sleep of Reason Produces Monsters*, which he worked on intermittently between 1793 and 1799. She remarks upon its fundamental ambiguity. Does it mean that monsters rush in when reason is off its guard? Does it mean that reason's own dreams are full of monsters? Or, more dramatically, does it mean that the so-called reasonable man is mad without realizing it? For Warner, the ambiguity is essential to the impact it produces. Nor should we forget Goya's feverish, incongruous imagination. For the point of the grotesque is the mixed sense of horror and derision, amusement and fright (*NGB* 254ff). In fear and disgust, we are never far from laughter and derision. The capacity for 'making mock' complements the capacity for plumbing the depths of fear.

Within the modern horror film tradition, we have seen the development of the 'late grotesque'. This is comparatively recent. A director such as Hitchcock, schooled in cinematic tradition, makes sure to construct a gripping story, informed by psychological knowledge, even though he may incorporate scenes of notorious violence, as with *Psycho* (1960). However, with the cinema that is labelled 'postmodernist', the violence is gratuitous, and the response induced is self-consciously frivolous:

> Quentin Tarantino crystallizes this contemporary grotesque humour of mockery in the scene in *Pulp Fiction* (1994) when Vincent Vega (John Travolta) kills the passenger in the back seat by mistake, bespatters the car with blood and gore and bits of brains, and then can only think about how on earth he and his hit-man (Samuel L. Jackson) are going to clean up the mess. The disparity between the callous, domestic trivia of their anxieties and the magnitude of the horror is appallingly funny – it induces the new laughter of what I have called the late grotesque. (*NGB* 260)

Warner generalizes as neutrally as possible from such examples: 'Laughter greets these entertainments: a new kind of rancid sympathy. The monstrous are not strangers, after all, but the appalling potential of human evil' (*NGB* 261). However, there is surely an implicit critique of the aesthetic and moral poverty of such works, even while she acknowledges that we need to be able to find our bearings in the world they represent. This world is 'mock' in the sense of being endlessly artificial; and it 'makes mock' of experiences which have hitherto been treated as extremely disturbing. We need a sense of the past if we are not to be beguiled by the fads of the present.

But Warner's main concern here is not to condemn the shallow sensationalism of fashionable artefacts. Her wider interest in Part Three of the book is the very nature of laughter. In chapter 15, 'On the Paltriness of Things' (the title of which is derived from a statement by Longinus, 'ridicule is an amplification of the paltriness of things'), Warner takes stock of her developing thesis:

> A theme of this book has been a contradiction at the heart of human responses to fear: the processes by which people seek to undo enemy power simultaneously make it visible. In other words, the drive to define and delimit 'home', to name and circumscribe the abode and the milieu to which one belongs and where one feels safe, leads to naming and defining things – and people – out there beyond the fence on the other side of the perimeter wire. Humour takes part in this making of likenesses and differences. (*NGB* 328)

But is humour benign or malign? Warner quotes a variety of authorities, including the poet Baudelaire, the philosopher Bergson and the anthropologist Mary Douglas. As one might expect, her own position is ambivalent, in keeping with the very ambiguity that laughter involves. On the one hand, it could be seen as a good way of binding the social group together, or – equally valid – a means by which the individual resists social control. On the other hand, it could be seen as satanic, as an indication of how far we have fallen from the dignity of paradise.

Warner seems to favour the kind of humour which subverts oppressive hierarchy and which transforms the demonic into the ridiculous. Mixed messages are part of the joke. The very title of her book is itself a playful pun on a line from Louis MacNeice's poem 'Bagpipe Music': 'It's no go the Yogi-man' (*NGB* x). Thinking of that title, she here considers the example of the tactics adopted by black musicians in the southern USA. 'Boogieman', a term derived from 'bogeyman', was slang for blacks; jazz composers and performers recuperated the insult by defiantly playing what they called 'boogie-woogie'. This is a tactic to be celebrated: humour defuses aggression. But we must not forget that aggression can disguise itself as humour, as is illustrated by the popularity of racist jokes. In such cases, 'laughter can fail to soothe or bring relief; it can raise the very devils that it imagined needed holding at bay' (*NGB* 348).

In racism, as in much social consolidation, the act of unification is achieved by exclusion. What is excluded is a figure who serves as projection of the repressed anxieties of the members of the group. Here we approach the subject of the scapegoat – a thoroughly traditional one (it dates back to the book of Leviticus and beyond) but especially relevant to contemporary experience. In a lengthy epilogue to *No Go the Bogeyman*, Warner tries to relate this phenomenon to the themes she has addressed over nearly 400 pages:

> Scapegoating functions to expel from a community the profound terrors it experiences about its own members' behaviour. ... Bogey-men make us look at the features of our own strangeness. Joyce Carol Oates has made the point, in her essay on contemporary forms of the grotesque: 'I take as the most profound mystery of our human experience the fact that, though we each exist subjectively ... this

"subjectivity" is inaccessible, thus unreal, and mysterious, to *others*. And the obverse – all *others* are, in the deepest sense, *strangers*.' To show the emptiness of fear, to identify its pernicious workings and prevent them, must be part of any system of education and justice. Yet the problem remains that the impulse to find a culprit, however innocent, lies deeply rooted in human psychology and culture. (*NGB* 377)

We have moved from childish fears of being threatened by an ogre to the very real suffering of thousands upon thousands of adults, as victims of prejudice and persecution. Admittedly, our survey has been a somewhat circuitous journey; admittedly, many more issues have been raised en route than have been fully dealt with (the nature of evil being the most glaring example). But this book is typical in that Warner has moved effortlessly from the most personal, intimate situation (being sung to by one's mother) to the arena of international politics. Again, though, the subject is not explored in the depth one might expect. It is only with the appearance of her next novel that one realizes that the epilogue to *No Go* has been a rehearsal for some of its themes. Certainly, the novel – a work of scope even more ambitious than that of the one just considered – is a sustained celebration of that most familiar of contemporary scapegoats, the refugee.

*****

The Leto Bundle (2001) is based on the myth of the female Titan who couples with Zeus, thereafter becoming pregnant. Zeus promises to protect her, but soon abandons her when his wife Hera makes objections. Leto is forced into exile and condemned to wander throughout the world before she can give birth to the twins Apollo and Artemis. Warner's interest in the myth is the opportunity it provides for embellishment over time and space, tracing the plight of the refugee through the centuries as she wanders from country to country. Thus, the novel moves from antiquity through modernity to postmodern-ity, out of ancient 'Lycania' into contemporary 'Albion'. In doing so, history itself is mythologized, even as the original myth of Leto is historicized.

Warner provides a convenient 'Chronology' in note form at the end of the book, set out in the neutral, secular mode of dating that scholars increasingly prefer to the Christian. In

'Lycania', it tells us, a cult site of the Titaness was founded between 400 and 350 BCE ('before the common era'). Between 325 and 350 CE ('the common era'), 'The Letoniast Version' was set down on papyrus: this was the earliest written version of the myth. We read on: '425–475 CE: Cartonnage or face mask was made for tomb occupant; linen bands inscribed' (*LB* 406). This cryptic piece of information hinges on the ambiguities and uncertainties which inform the plot of the novel. Who was this occupant? If Leto was a mythic figure, then it could not have been her; but of course, if there was a cult of Leto, the devotees would have wanted to believe her body was inside the tomb. Add to this tension of possibilities the complication that in 620 CE the necropolis was buried by a landslide, and we have the makings of a mystery which might interweave with the history which we are about to have recounted to us. The very way those two words, 'history' and 'mystery', rhyme might even have its own resonance. *The Leto Bundle* is to a large extent a novel about the way human beings cannot help but search for significance in apparent coincidence and in chance discoveries.

The chronology provided is there as a reference point, but the novel actually begins in the present, in the land of 'Albion'. The name is mythic in its own right: numerous literary works, including some plays of Shakespeare, have referred to England by that name. In particular, it is associated with the prophetic poems of the great Romantic, William Blake: for him it is not only a land but also an archetypal human being, the primal man whose task is to wake up from the sleep of materialism and ignorance in order to discover his own spiritual identity (Blake, 233ff). How much of the Blakean resonance needs recognizing in order to appreciate this novel it is hard to estimate. Suffice it to say for the moment that the visionary poet is important to the extent that many of the names of characters and places are inspired by him; but we might be in danger of spoiling the reading experience if we chase after every possible allusion. The city of 'Enoch' or London does not appear to be Blakean, even though a character named Enoch, inspired by that in the Bible, appears in Blake's prophecies: it is more likely that it is named after Enoch Powell, the Conservative politician famed for demanding in the late 1960s that immigrants of different ethnic origin from the native English should be repatriated. However we interpret the name of the city, it is there that the 'Museum of Albion' is located, and it is that institution which is the focus of much of the intrigue of the novel. Elsewhere, Blake is a broadly imaginative presence rather than a specific cultural influence – with the notable exception of a character named Gramercy Poule, a folk-rock singer whose song lyrics are directly inspired by him. But the Blakean dimension of the novel as a whole is a theme we may return to once we have our narrative bearings.

The museum, we soon learn, is frequently visited by one Kim McQuay, a dedicated primary school teacher who is enthusiastic, not to say obsessive, about the contemporary relevance of ancient myths. In particular, he is fascinated by 'the Leto Bundle'. But what exactly is a 'bundle'? In the catalogue accompanying the exhibition for which she acted as curator in 1996, *The Inner Eye: Art Beyond the Visible*, Warner elaborated on this very notion:

> Imagine a bundle ceremony among one of the indigenous tribes in Canada – Cree or Blackfoot. ... [The bundles] contain scraps of possessions, rags, objects, nothing of intrinsic value, but they are thought to be imbued with the identity of the family to whom they belong, and, as recovered family totems, they are received and unwrapped in great solemnity during the ritual. (*IE* 18–19)

The Leto 'bundle' is similar: it is a collection of oddments, all of which seem to have some connection with a sacred cult. Even when the museum has to admit that its initial marketing ploy of using the name 'Helen', suggesting that it has in its possession the body of Helen of Troy, has been mistaken, and that all they can boast is a motley assemblage of items associated with the myth of Leto, Kim and others continue to visit again and again. Apart from the schoolteacher, these visitors consist largely of vagrants and beggars, the needy and the vulnerable: those whom Franz Fanon called 'the wretched of the earth'. In Kim's words, 'she truly is the goddess of diaspora'; she is the 'embodiment of the dispersed and the drowned' (*LB* 120). Every generation has recognized her, but it is only now that her full significance may be grasped. Why? Because it is now that the world is witnessing a catastrophic displacement of human communities, each of which consists of individuals just like the exiled Leto, wandering from land to land seeking refuge. So profound is this significance that Kim has started a movement known as 'History Starts With Us' – the 'us' referring to the scapegoats of globalization, the victims of international capital. Someone else who is interested in this idea, someone who is undoubtedly privileged but also dissatisfied with her status and wealth, is Gramercy Poule. She is surprised to discover that Kim has published on his 'HSWU' website an apparent declaration by Leto: 'I am the angel of the present time'. Not only does this sum up the goddess's relevance, but it is also a variation on a line from one of her own songs. Precluding the possibility of plagiarism, it would seem that Leto really is beginning to speak through many voices, and make herself known in many ways. At one point, she is even referred to defiantly by a devotee as 'Our Lady' (*LB* 97).

In a sense, then, *The Leto Bundle* is Warner's fictional revisiting of some of the ideas first put forward in *Alone of All Her Sex*. The contemporary dedication to Leto which she describes might be seen as a secular counterpart to 'the myth and cult of the Virgin Mary'. If traditionally Catholics looked to 'Our Lady' for succour in times of need, now it seems that in our secular age this function might be taken over, at least as far as those in extreme need are concerned, by the goddess who was herself dispossessed, exiled and persecuted. The only deity who can unify those scattered by global conflict is one who takes on the role of the scapegoat. In the Jewish faith, that function was forced upon an actual animal, driven out into the wilderness in order to relieve the tribe of the burden of its guilt. In Christianity itself, Jesus willingly assumed the role, becoming figuratively 'the lamb of God who takest away the sins of the world'. Warner's variation on the theme involves shifting the role from a male to a female deity, from Jesus to Mary (the latter being virtually divine, in the popular Christian imagination of the Middle Ages and early modernity), and then renaming her so that she becomes thoroughly secular in status. Leto is the recognizable icon of all victims of this postmodern, globalized era, in which nothing is sacred – paradoxically, since an icon is an image that has traditionally been regarded as holy.

Her journey, beginning with her abandonment by Zeus, takes her through the region of Lycania, as it will be called: its name derives from the name of the wolf, Lycia, who shelters her and her twins, known here as Phoebus and Phoebe. Leto has affinities with the animal kingdom, and even – given her ability to live hand to mouth in caves and dugouts – the earth itself. But she cannot stay within this sphere of experience, and must venture forth into history. Thus, the next major episode of the novel sees her making her way through the barbaric era of the Christian crusades, waged against the 'infidels' in the Middle East from the eleventh to the thirteenth centuries. Of course, in *The Leto Bundle*, the names and events have been heavily adapted. The disputes are between the 'Orphiri' (Muslim), the Lazuli (Byzantine) and the Enochite (English Christian) residents of an area known as 'Cademas-la-Jolie'. In 1165 (Warner's chronology, though fictional, is exact), an Orphiri leader called Cunmar becomes vice-procurator of the fortified outpost established in that area in 998. Cademas-la-Jolie is precariously occupied by Orphiri, Lazuli and Enochite communities, with Cunmar in the reluctant role of peacemaker. His mind is frequently on other things: in particular, he adopts a 5-year-old girl named Laetitia, only to fall in love with her when she approaches womanhood. This female, who is the most recent incarnation of Leto in the course of her spatio-temporal journey, is on the verge of marrying Cunmar when his wife and son, outraged at his behaviour, decide to have her murdered. However, the servants cannot bring themselves to carry out their instructions, and they leave Leto and her twins outside the citadel's walls to take their chances. Members of the convent in which she was raised, believing the mother to be dead, declare her a martyr.

We now move forward several centuries, to find Leto and her children as stowaways on the HMS Shearwater, which is travelling back to Enoch after Sir Giles Skipwith's excavations in Lycania of 1839–41. The ironies should not escape us. Firstly, Sir Giles has in his possession the 'Leto Bundle' at the same time as the ship has on board Leto herself. Warner hints that the reality of the eternal wanderer's suffering is becoming over-shadowed by the fascination with artefacts associated with her. Secondly, when Leto is discovered, Sir Giles regards her as an intriguing example of 'primitive' culture, which for him is the antithesis of the 'classical' civilization which is his own scholarly interest. Warner seems to be offering some incidental satire at

110

the expense of the kind of positivist mythography which became fashionable in the nineteenth century, culminating in Sir James Frazer, who notoriously regarded human progress as a triumphal movement from 'savage' magic and religion to 'rational' science. In either case, Leto is the victim.

However, Sir Giles's intentions are benign. It is not he, but the ship's cook, Strugwell, who wishes to exploit her. Smuggling her and the twins off the *HMS Shearwater* at night, with the enforced assistance of the cabin boy, Teal (whose memoirs provide much of our material here), he sells her to Ibn Hamiz the merchant. Later, Teal deserts ship, having stolen the money which Strugwell received, and goes to help the captives escape. Typically, the constant victim is helped by someone whose own lowly position means that he instinctively recognizes their affinity.

But Leto escapes only to be immersed in the wars and international confusion of the present day. Her journey, and so her ordeal, goes on. It takes her into the heart of 'Tirzah'. Before registering the historical parallels, we should perhaps note that in the Song of Solomon, Tirzah signifies physical beauty, more specifically sexual attraction. While we have said that the Blakean symbolism is not consistently used, perhaps we do need to know that for Blake Tirzah is the maker of the physical body, the 'Mother of my Mortal part'. This latter phrase comes from the cryptic poem which appears towards the end of the *Songs of Experience*. 'To Tirzah' is commonly interpreted as representing the Gnostic aspect of Blake's vision, which sees matter as intrinsically evil: the spirit has to dissociate itself from the dross of the flesh, here represented by a sinister maternal figure (Blake, 30). We may legitimately surmise that Warner is making the allusion ironically, since *The Leto Bundle* is precisely about the denial of the rights of a mother, whose only offence is to want to survive and to protect her children. Warner knows, of course, that for every demonized woman, Blake offers a positive ideal: the most positive of all is Jerusalem herself, the emanation of Albion himself; but she could hardly have used that name for a war-torn city in the Balkans. For that is where we now find Leto. Tirzah is very like Sarajevo, capital of Bosnia, which was the main focus of conflict during the war of 1991–5, occasioned by the violent nationalism of the Serbs, under the presidency of the notorious Slobodan Milošević. If one has previously been thinking of Blake's demonic female, one cannot help but reflect here on how he might depict such a man as this: surely as an angry, jealous father of his people, guided by a distorted use of reason, and dedicated to the suppression of those with different customs and beliefs.

The imaginary war centred around Tirzah occurs rather earlier than the historical conflict between the Serbians and the Bosnians: Warner tells us it runs from 1970 to 1975. But the parallels are clear, and they only enforce the contemporary relevance of the novel. For it was with the Balkan catastrophe that western Europeans became acutely aware of the phenomenon of 'ethnic cleansing' and the displacement of whole cultures, right on their doorstep. Certainly, in terms of the novel's spatio-temporal structure, we may say that Leto is approaching our own world, having travelled westwards from antiquity through modernity. But her ordeal only intensifies: her daughter Phoebe is flayed alive by a military explosion, which entails Leto in a desperate search for medical help. Bewildered and exhausted, she can no longer look after both twins, so she agrees to have Phoebus adopted by childless Enochites.

Coming even closer to our time and place, we finally see Leto arriving in Albion, where she becomes known by the name of 'Ella'. It is here, posing as a hotel maid in order to get a place to sleep (a laundry cupboard, to be exact), she encounters the singer Gramercy Poule, who is on tour. Gramercy decides to take responsibility for this woman, recognizing something exceptional in her character. She gives her a job running the animal sanctuary attached to her estate. Meanwhile Ella is able to visit Enoch and seek advice from a council for refugees, hoping to trace Phoebus. Of course, her determination, while impressive to Gramercy, is not associated in the latter's mind with the endurance of the goddess Leto herself, whom the singer wishes to celebrate in a film. This project brings her into contact with Kim McQuay, founder of 'History Starts With Us', and also with Hortense ('Hetty') Fernly, a curator at the Museum of Albion with special responsibility for the 'Leto Bundle'. A love triangle involving Kim, Gramercy and Hortense is dramatized in the last few chapters, though it is never allowed to overshadow the central narrative of Leto's search for her son, for her place of sanctuary, and ultimately for her very identity.

Eventually, Ella sees Kim on his visit to Gramercy's mansion, and she knows he is the same Phoebus whom she had reluctantly given up for adoption. However, Kim is shortly after killed in a violent incident in the playground of his school, in which he tries to prevent one of his pupils being kidnapped by a stranger. Whether this tragedy results from a feud between rival gangs, or perhaps rival racial communities, is unclear: the point is that Kim dies a martyr's death. Leto, who has lost the son whom she has nurtured over continents and centuries, disappears in despair. The only reminder of her presence is by ancient association: at a harvest fair, her daughter Phoebe appears in the company of 'Lucy' the wolf; this episode recalls the beginning of the long search for refuge, when Lycia came to the aid of Leto and the twins. Again, the occasion of the festival itself – harvest – is a reminder of the cycle of nature going on, which Leto's recurrence surely parallels. The novel closes with, firstly, a 'threnody' which apostrophizes Leto as an eternal mythic figure, and, secondly, an epilogue in which Gramercy puts an advertisement in *Voice of the Streets* (Warner's equivalent of the *Big Issue*) asking for help in ascertaining Ella's whereabouts. Leto may be eternal, but she is also eternally elusive, and easily overlooked. As Ella herself has speculated earlier in the novel: 'The remnant ... we are always the remnant ... we are the disappeared, made invisible' (*LB* 264).

Warner's novel asks us to speculate whether her account of this representative of the remnant constitutes a coherent narrative: that is, whether the myth of Leto can make sense of a seemingly random and discontinuous series of events. In an e-mail exchange between Kim and Hortense, he maintains that it does, that there is one continuous story implicit in the Leto bundle itself. And he insists, in the hasty, almost garbled language of internet communication, that the story is being told even now:

> when you're looking into space you're looking into time   what you see happened a long time ago   it's called lookback time   that's like Leto and her two babies   they happened a long time ago but their presence in the light is coming nearer all the time   the actual speed is one foot a billionth of a second not too difficult to remember   it was there and now it's reached us through the bundle in the tomb.

(*LB* 162)

Little does he know at this stage that he will become part of the myth, by virtue of his death. After the murder in the playground, Hortense, whom he has come to know and love as Hetty, reflects on its significance, in the light of her knowledge of myths of male deities who meet violent ends:

> And Hetty thought of the cults of fallen heroes, of dying gods in their mothers' laps, of the founding blood of martyrs: the brutal logic of sacrifice. Would the plot never stop repeating? Would it ever be possible to start again, as Kim had wanted, and delete the old files of history? 'It is ghastly,' she said quietly, 'and I wish with all my heart that it weren't so. But Kim is dead, and maybe that makes it his story now.' (*LB* 388)

What we have learnt, rather, is that Leto's story comprehends all other tales of suffering, dispossession and victimization. She is the appropriate mythic figure for our age because we no longer believe in regal triumph, only in common tragedy. Kim was right to an extent: history may not 'start with us', but it is about 'us', if we extend 'us' to comprehend 'the wretched of the earth'.

In assessing *The Leto Bundle*, one may be put off by the rather ponderous structure and symbolism; but one can hardly deny its power as an inclusive vision. As in Warner's previous fiction, we see how intimately past, present and future are interwoven; but more than ever, we are aware of a broad and deep compassion, willing to explore and celebrate those whom 'History' (that grand narrative which we designate by a capital H) has markedly ignored. Again, the tension between the experience and the representation of women informs this work; but what is new is the attempt to dignify that experience by a defiant rewriting of mythology. In antiquity, Leto was an incidental figure; here she becomes central. In contemporary experience, a female refugee might not merit much attention in her own right; here she is the centre of a myth for the postmodern age – and beyond.

We might put this last point another way by saying that a movement that began over two and a half centuries ago, in the midst of modernity, has re-emerged all the stronger. In the glossary of *The Inner Eye*, Warner's entry for William Blake reads:

'prophet of the Counter-Enlightenment and champion of the imagination' (*IE* 31). What was the Counter-Enlightenment? Warner's entry reads: 'Term coined by Isaiah Berlin, adopted by E. P. Thompson and others, to characterize heterogeneous opposition from mid-C17 to the cult of reason; embracing various romantic, vitalist, psychic and spiritual approaches to knowledge, and ranging from Giambattista Vico's study of myths, Blake's private mythologies, to today's New Age' (*IE* 34). We have already noted the possibility that a Blakean code underlies Warner's composition of this novel, though our brief exposition has not provided the opportunity of cracking it. However, *The Leto Bundle* is surely in keeping with the more radical side of Blake's vision, that which resists the domination of human life by 'Urizen', god of rational calculation. We recall that in *The Book of Urizen*, this false deity proclaims: 'One command, one joy, one desire,/ One curse, one weight, one measure / One king, one God, one law' (Blake, 72). Resistance to this sterile authoritarianism may today take the form of fashionable 'New Age' dabbling – the kind of interest that would lead a Gramercy Poule to seek credibility by aligning herself with Blake – but it is to Warner's credit that this novel reveals to us a more responsible, and perhaps more human, alternative. The myth of Leto, as dramatized here, is perhaps the legitimate myth for our time, as globalization renders the many more vulnerable than ever to the monolithic might of the few.

7

Fantastic Metamorphoses and *Murderers I Have Known*

We come now to Warner's very latest works, published while this book was nearing completion. Thus, what might have been a chapter of retrospective summation will have to be a chapter of prospective speculation. But this is probably all to the good, as Warner's is above all a dynamic art.

As has been the case previously, she has produced a work of fiction in close proximity to a work of mythography, with considerable overlapping of interests. *Murderers I Have Known and other stories* (2002) is a collection of fictional pieces, some of them commissioned during the 1990s and some of them written specially for the volume. *Fantastic Metamorphoses, Other Worlds: Ways of Telling the Self* (2002) is based on the Clarendon Lectures which Warner delivered in the autumn of 2001, and it relates to an exhibition called *Metamorphing* which she co-curated with Sarah Bakewell at the Science Museum in London in the autumn and winter of 2002. Both books are about the need for change.

Turning to the latter first, we see Warner going right back to the origins of art, to consider the relationship between reality and representation. For the 'metamorphosis' in which she is interested is above all a process of the imagination: after all, the word 'metaphor' comes from the same etymological root. In other words, 'transformation' is above all a trope. The most famous work to celebrate the capacity to imagine what might be, or to re-imagine what is, is of course Ovid's *Metamorphoses*, which Warner begins by acknowledging as a lifelong inspiration to herself. That wonderful compendium of myths and legends is certainly a work of compelling fantasy, and it certainly opens out

116

to us 'other worlds' which transform our perception of our own. The image of Acteon being changed into a stag after seeing Diana bathing, of Arachne into a spider for daring to challenge Minerva in a weaving competition, of Daphne into a bay-tree to prevent Apollo taking her virginity: these are endlessly absorbing images. The very idea that such bodily changes can be made so easily, that they are not exceptions to the order of the universe but rather examples of its never-ending cyclical replenishment, may seem disturbing at first. In which case, we might want to interpret such events wholly negatively, as threats to the self which we feel we ought to assert and defend. But Warner proposes that that is the specific legacy of Judaeo-Christianity, which has regarded a stable human identity as sacrosanct: metamorphosis, as in Dante's vision in hell, is seen in wholly demonic terms. Ovid, on the other hand, invoking Pythagoras, can affirm: 'All things are always changing, / But nothing dies. ... / As the pliant wax / Is stamped with new designs, and is no longer / What once it was, but changes form, and still / Is pliant wax, so do I teach that spirit / Is evermore the same, though passing always / To ever-changing bodies' (Book 15, ll. 165–8). Quoting these lines, Warner comments: 'The blurring here between art and nature, as in the imagery of wax moulding (as used for sculpture casting), in order to convey the migrating forms of life, recurs in the long poem with significant frequency: in this vision, metamorphosis is the principle of organic vitality as well as the pulse in the body of art' (*FMOW* 2).

Thus, art more naturally inclines to Ovid's prolixity and plurality than to Judaeo-Christian restraint. But what interests her is that the tension between the two notions of the self, the Ovidian and the biblical, has continued to inform the western concept of character. As technology makes transformation of the self more and more possible, and more and more pervasive, we do not know which side of the equation to come down upon. Cyborgs, mutants, replicants and aliens inhabit our popular entertainment industry, but also seem more and more likely to form part of our experience: witness the growth of cosmetic surgery, cloning and artificial insemination. We do not know whether to be repelled or intrigued. Warner, sensitive to our ambivalence, guides us through this minefield in the way she knows best: by providing cultural bearings from myth and history, and by demonstrating how art can offer new 'ways of telling the self' beyond mere physical manipulation.

In her introduction to the book, where she reflects upon her research for the lectures on which it is based, she recalls that 'through my reading of fantastic literature, I intimated that tales of metamorphosis often arose in spaces (temporal, geographical, and mental) that were crossroads, cross-cultural zones, points of interchange on the intricate connective tissue of communications between cultures' (*FMOW* 17). Thus, notions of transformation relate to 'the transmigration of stories': 'It is no accident that fairy tales were first written down, for example, all round the edge of the Mediterranean, in Egypt and in the greater ports of Venice and Naples, and travelled along trade routes far and wide', for 'it is characteristic of metamorphic writing to appear in transitional places and at the confluence of traditions and civilizations' (*FMOW* 17–18). Thus, ways of telling the self are inseparable from ways of telling and transmitting stories: individual identity is far more of an effect of narrative, culture and history than it is their cause. The four lectures, then, cover four possible permutations of personal identity which have recurred over the centuries, depending on the prevailing assumptions and attitudes of the day. (For the record, these are, respectively, 'Mutating', 'Hatching', 'Splitting' and 'Doubling'.)

Two concepts which she discovered in the course of her research, Warner tells us, helped her explore the notion of otherness which is implicit in her title. When we speak of 'other worlds', we often think in terms of pure fantasy; but we also form strange images of real, existing cultures that happen to be alien to our own. We know that Warner has always been alert to that oppressive tendency which Said calls 'orientalism', but here she finds some scope for a more positive view of the colonial experience by way of Peter Hulme's idea of 'congeners'. These Warner defines as 'materials through which one culture interacts with and responds to another, conductors of energies that may themselves not be apparent or directly palpable in the resulting transformations' (*FMOW* 18). In other words, an oppressed culture may have an imaginative impact upon the oppressing culture which eludes or exceeds the material process of imperial exploitation. Here the second concept, Peter Lamborn Wilson's 'positive shadow', comes into play: 'He introduces it, in reference to the Europeans who "turned Turk", to characterize the ways colonized or repudiated cultures can still exercise a fascination, a "perfume of seduction" over their new masters, and thereby produce a series of reciprocal transformations' (*FMOW* 19–20).

If we seek an example of the process by which cultures interact, so that the very way of imagining the self can be transformed at an historical crossroads, we might consider the figure of the zombie, to which Warner devotes much of her third lecture, 'Splitting'. She suggests that it is a perfect example of the encounter with the 'other': in this case, the settlement of Africa and the Americas by early modern Europeans opened them up to new images of identity. Among the inhabitants of those lands the settlers discovered the idea of the 'Zambi', or deity, represented by a chief or leader to whom the people would willingly surrender their souls – allowing themselves to be 'possessed', it seemed. Robert Southey, during his researches on West Indian religion, decided that 'Zambi' meant 'the Devil'. But his friend Samuel Taylor Coleridge corrected this notion, indicating that it meant, rather, '*a* devil': that is, a Platonic 'daemon' or indwelling vital principle. In doing so, the great Romantic poet helped initiate a major transformation of sensibility. Instead of dismissing the convictions of others from 'the point of view of Christian monotheism, which holds all other gods to be diabolical', he allowed scope for a 'plural, Neoplatonist polytheism', so that Zambi, as 'daemon', need be characterized as 'neither exclusively earthbound, nor celestial, moral nor immoral, intrinsically malign nor benign' (*FMOW* 150).

But the implications of his openness to the other do not stop there: 'Coleridge's poetry exhibits the inversion, with regard to the idea of soul-death, and he makes the first declared link between the West Indies and a new psychology of the supernatural' (*FMOW* 150). With him, the image of the zombie begins to occupy the European mind, figuring forth its shifting sense of the unknown, the uncanny, the paranormal. For now the focus is on the psyche itself – on the soul, or 'daemon' – and on the fear of its alienation from the body. Consider 'The Rime of the Ancient Mariner': 'after the death of the albatross, the doomed ship moves, bewitched, laden with its "ghastly crew", all of them living dead whose sounds and looks deepen the narrator's spellbound condition' (*FMOW* 153). The state being described is, Warner surmises, the internal effect of colonization on the colonizer. How can this be? Her insight is that the image of the zombie, at first confined to the colonized and later misunderstood as demonic 'possession', now provides a means of depicting a pervasive and destabilizing sense of 'dispossession'. This most obviously describes the immediate impact on the victim of colonialism, namely brutal, physical displacement; but it may also describe the psychological condition of the perpetrator, whose mind suffers the repressed awareness of the disaster wreaked by endless expansion and exploitation. There is, then, a 'lineage of hauntings' which animates much western culture from the Gothic novel, via Jean Rhys's *Wide Sargasso Sea*, to Angela Carter's powerfully 'daemonic' fiction. Nor should we forget such classic horror films as *I Walked with a Zombie* – which is, like Rhys's novel, a rewriting of Charlotte Brontë's *Jane Eyre* (*FWOM* 122–3, 154–60).

The kind of process just described may seem wholly negative at first glance, but Warner's point is that it has enabled the crisis of the self, at a moment of cultural 'congening', to be articulated imaginatively: in that sense, the 'shadow' is 'positive'. This, indeed, is what art has always done: open up the ego to a larger mode of being, both external and internal. Thus, the theme of the 'double', the subject of the fourth lecture, is central to the nature of aesthetics, though specific manifestations may vary from age to age. On the one hand, the figure of the other, the doppelgänger, so dominant in nineteenth-century novels such as *Frankenstein* and *Dr Jekyll and Mr Hyde*, may offer the threat of estrangement from self. On the other hand, the very idea of 'doubling' also 'solicits hopes and dreams for yourself, of a possible becoming different while remaining the same person, of escaping the bounds of self, of aspiring to the polymorphous perversity of infants, in Freud's phrase, which in some ways mimics the protean energies of the metamorphic gods' (*FMOW* 164–5).

Not that Warner has ever relied entirely on psychoanalysis to understand the rich paradoxes of the human mind, or of art. Here she reminds us that centuries ago Shakespeare offered to act as our guide to that 'magic' which allows us to represent ourselves by way of illusion. It is no coincidence, she suggests, that such insights paralleled the invention of the 'magic lantern':

When Prospero talks of his 'insubstantial pageant', it is hard not to imagine stagecraft of an optical variety. Indeed, in his famous speech, he says, 'We are such stuff as dreams are made on' (*The Tempest*, IV.i.14ff) – could that 'on' suggest that dreams appear on something, on the screen of fantasy, the scrim on which shadow puppets play? Theatrical illusion offers an analogy to the spectral conjurings of enchanters as well as the phantasms of haunted minds, to Goya's nightmare of reason. (*FMOW* 170)

For the capacity to form visions – to create images of ourselves as other, or of non-existent phenomena as existent – was being addressed with a newly technical vocabulary in early modernity: 'The inner eye, or eye of the imagination, was conceived as a kind of projector, onto the screen of fantasy hovering somewhere beyond the back of the head' (*FMOW* 171).

In a fascinating train of scholarly speculation, Warner traces the influence of the Oxford Neoplatonist philosopher Robert Fludd (whose *Of the Other World* was published only a few years after Shakespeare's late romances were performed) on the early experiments with magic-lantern slide-shows. What was represented at these was chiefly spectral in nature: ghosts, devils, souls burning in the fires of hell, and so forth. Ingeniously, Warner conjectures that Shakespeare had always understood the paradox of 'doubling', which unites artistic representation and demonic disorientation: 'Image magic frequently proceeds by mimesis and replication; verbal spells also use imitation and doubling to achieve their ends.' What is projected is 'the shadow not the substance, the double not the original'. Appropriately enough, she reminds us of a famous line: ' "Double double toil and trouble," chant the witches in *Macbeth* over their cauldron (*Macbeth* IV.i)' (*FMOW* 167). But Shakespeare knew too the necessity for art to articulate the undeniable duality of our existence: 'In the *Dream* Theseus talks of "shaping fantasies", "aery nothing", to which "the madman, the lover, and the poet/ Give a local habitation and a name ..." (V.i.5–17). Reversing Prospero's metaphor, Theseus also says that actors themselves are "shadows": Puck repeats this in the play's envoi ("If we shadows have offended", V.i.423ff)' (*FMOW* 170). Whether it is the actors who are shadowing us or it is we who are acting as if in a pageant, the insight is the same: what each of us thinks of as the real 'me' is neither essential nor stable, but depends on 'ways of telling' – or, here, projecting – 'the self'. Those ways are cultural, and so – paradoxically – collective.

But what, then, of our contemporary culture, and its attitude to metamorphosis? Warner sees the danger of transformation being confined to a cult of bodily perfection, as is evident in the flourishing of 'the cosmetic and surgical industries' (*FMOW* 210). But if we are interested in imaginative transformation, then that will involve storytelling, informed by the legacy of mythology. For the tales recounted by Ovid were attempts to negotiate between the fear of change and the need for change: if we read him aright, then we should begin to worry when we are no longer capable of metamorphosis. In his great poem, a celebration of endless change, the worst fate is petrification, to be turned to stone by the gaze of the Gorgon. For stasis is a figure for the death of the creativity that moves the universe itself. This is true of the self, and it is also true of story itself. Warner lists several recent or contemporary writers who, she feels, have kept the spirit of metamorphosis alive, giving the ancient myths new and often startling relevance: among the poets, Ted Hughes, Seamus Heaney and Christopher Logue; among the novelists, A. S. Byatt, Salman Rushdie and Philip Pullman. In her Epilogue, she remarks: 'This list of writers could be added to, of course; it is the lineage within which I would like to place myself, as someone who writes fiction and thinks about the life of stories' (*FMOW* 211). This modest affirmation of her own contribution leads her on to her conclusion, in which she asserts without reserve the importance of keeping narrative alive:

> One of the things that we want from stories, it seems, is orientation, with regard to the powers that we imagine govern our destinies, call them gods or fate or providence or chaos or relativity. ... It would be stupid to suggest stories inevitably enlighten; but stories do offer a way of imagining alternatives, mapping possibilities, exciting hope, warding off danger by forestalling it, casting spells of order on the unknown ahead. (*FMOW* 212)

Warner's *Fantastic Metamorphoses, Other Worlds* makes a good case for resisting stasis and embracing change.

*****

It may be said, in the light of the above, that many of the stories in *Murderers I Have Known* are about the dangers of petrification. Their protagonists have been rendered immobile, in some sense, and need to find a way of beginning to move once more. In 'Natural Limits', Candace, widow of Tom, realizes that she should never have married and that she had for some time been resentful of him: being 'used up' himself, he had effectively restricted her own growth also. Now she is afraid of life, feeling ill at ease in the world. She is also burdened by guilt because, having been estranged from Tom for some time, she had failed to attend his funeral. Persuaded by her friend to visit Cologne, she views a strange mosaic of bones on the ceiling of the cathedral crypt: they belonged to St Ursula and her fellow-virgins, long ago murdered by Huns, but their elaborate formation is still curiously impressive. Later, in the monastery, she is guided round a small 'Museum of Likeness and Presence', which is the 'cabinet of curiosities' established by an art restorer, Gervase Mendoza, where she is presented with a bizarre spectacle:

> 'You cannot photograph it,' said Gervase. 'It's an image which has no reflection. Because it's not made of light, but only of deeper degrees of shadow. So the only place you can see it is here, and in this darkness. ... It is the true likeness of a soul in paradise, caught permanently as an impression in the air, in the same way as you see matter dance in the rays of the sun.' (*MIHK* 26–7)

This magic lantern show, in keeping with Warner's comments in *Fantastic Metamorphoses*, forces Candace to reflect on the relationship between reality and representation, truth and illusion, the natural and the supernatural. Her own limited identity, which has been such a dead weight for so long, begins to find release, to float free in the realm of imagination. The spectacles she has seen in the cathedral and the museum effectively de-petrify her. She is able to embrace death and life simultaneously.

And so, when she gets home, she remembers the urn that her husband had arranged to be sent to her, and decides to confront it at last. Preparing a salad from odd items left in her refrigerator, she incorporates their contents in her snack: she 'took some of Tom's dust and ashes and sprinkled them like pepper on the mayonnaise; she loaded her fork and bit carefully, reverently, expecting a tart, metal pungency, something like semen but dry. The flavour was elusive, so she took another two dressed and seasoned leaves, but found that they tasted no different' (*MIHK* 28). We may infer that Candace has discovered that the 'taste' of her own life is equally 'elusive': that the 'natural limits' she has accepted are not as natural as she had assumed, but that nature, as in Ovid's perspective, is more marvellous than can ever be rationally understood. Only art – the mosaic of bones, the likeness of the soul in paradise, this story itself – can show us.

But art also has to show us how often we fail to open ourselves to marvels. The narrator of the volume's title story, 'Murderers I Have Known', has an obsession which may seem to spring from an over-active imagination, but rather results from a narrowing of vision, a restricting of potential. She is fixated on the idea of serial murderers, seeing them everywhere: again and again, she hears about one, or thinks she has met one, but identifying one proves elusive. The main character she tells us about is a rapist not a murderer: Johnnie Thompson, the 'Sussex Strangler', who used to do odd jobs for her father when she was young, has never actually killed any of his victims, despite threatening them with strangulation. This expressed desire to be acquainted with an agent of death is a morbid perversion of a repressed desire to live and to love. Her ex-stepmother Natalie, who has a new lover, is so obviously capable of carnal enjoyment that the narrator feels uncomfortable. At the end of the story, she goes to bed in the room she had slept in when she was younger, but is disturbed by a noise. Her head full of thoughts of murderers, she has to ask Natalie to investigate: it transpires that the noise had been made by a bat, clinging to the curtain of the window opposite the bed. This prompts her concluding meditation, in which she alludes to an influential work of art (one we have encountered before, discussed by Warner in *No Go the Bogeyman*), and in which she invokes Ovid:

> Bats are streaming from the head of the dreamer in Goya's famous etching, *The Sleep of Reason Produces Monsters*, and I realised that I was imagining things because the news about Johnnie Thompson had shaken me. I'm over that fear now, and he's in a high-security psychiatric prison waiting on the Home Secretary's pleasure. All the

same, I seem to remember that Psyche hears her phantom lover come like a wind in the night. He turns out to be god of love, Eros himself, in that fairy tale, and they have a little girl, eventually, called Pleasure.

Pleasure. Natalia knows about pleasure. I'd like to, as well. I'd open the window to let in a lover with the soft rush of the dark, if I didn't keep noticing things which make me fasten the latch instead. (*MIHK* 136–7)

Petrified by fear – of life, of death, of herself – the narrator can only see the male other as bogeyman or ogre. Her excessive rationality prevents her embracing both the light and the dark, both love and danger, both the soul and the body.

If the sleep of reason produces monsters, insomnia of imagination produces inertia. *Murderers I Have Known* contains a contemporary fairy tale in which a princess has to learn how to dream. 'Lullaby for an Insomniac Princess' was written as an occasional piece, in response to the music of John Woolrich; it would seem to be a variation on 'The Princess and the Pea'. Inheriting her incapacity to sleep from the king and queen, who suffered from it during the pregnancy, Imogen has become old before her time, because she has had so much of it: time to read, to reason, to worry. Hers is an excessively mature mind in a young person's body.

One day, a fowler calls at the palace. Initially, he upsets her by explaining that he traps songbirds; however, she is intrigued when he offers to escort her into the woods, so that she can hear the song of the female nightingale, which is much more beautiful than that of the male. Needless to say, the princess has read her Ovid and her Keats, so she can grasp intellectually the importance of the melody. She knows the terrible story of Philomel, raped and silenced by Tereus but still able, in the form of a nightingale, to sing of the offence for all to hear; she knows how far Keats in his ode wanted to be released from suffering and to merge with the beauty of that song. But it is only by pursuing the nightingale into the woods for herself that she can begin to come alive. For this can only happen, as with the Imogen of Shakespeare's romance, *Cymbeline*, by entering into darkness and death, and by allowing art to weave its spell. 'She tried to plunge on, but her limbs wouldn't obey her. She dropped down where she was, and the mulch was cool and soft.

She lay there till she could hear past her beating heart and harshly taken breath and sift the grounds of the wildwood; gradually the noises regrouped themselves, fell into patterns, subsided and settled' (*MIHK* 101). Then she hears the song. When she wakes, she is in her bed, and she is able to tell her parents that she has dreamt that she is just about to hear 'the most wonderful music in the world'. Realizing what has happened to her, that she has been given new life by the power of the imagination, she laughs, closes her eyes, and murmurs: 'Maybe if I go to sleep again, I'll hear some more' (*MIHK* 102).

*****

Perhaps we could say of Warner's work generally that it is a reminder of the need to retain the capacity to dream, to see ourselves and the world in a different perspective. In short, she demonstrates that mythically inspired literature may be, in Ricoeur's phrase, 'the bearer of other *possible worlds*'. Without myth, and without writers like Warner, we are condemned to stand still. Keeping the potential of past stories alive in the present, open to the future, is one of her main aims. As we noted in a previous chapter, she first glimpsed this possibility thanks to her Catholic upbringing, and in particular to that interpretation of the scriptures which we call 'typology'. For though, according to Warner, Judaeo-Christianity may value stability of the self, in its defensive stance against 'pagan' plurality of being, it is otherwise highly dynamic in its thinking: that is, it privileges time as the medium through which God effects human salvation. We have already quoted the article in which Warner reflects on her use of typology in *Indigo*. In an interview, she has summed up the principle with even more stress on temporal projection: 'there is an Old Covenant and a New Covenant, and the New Covenant exists as not just a continuum but as a recapitulation in an actual form of the promises of the past' (Tredell, 246–7). This typological strategy informs her view of all myth, whether biblical or 'pagan'; and it is evident in much of her fiction – not only *Indigo*, for example (which, as we know, takes *The Tempest* as its 'Old Covenant'), but also *Mermaids in the Basement* (where, amongst others, the stories of Moses, the Queen of Sheba and Ariadne are creatively revised).

In this light, we may infer that she is not impressed by contemporary culture in so far as it distorts that idea which we have seen to be so important to her, namely 'the presence of the past'. This is too often reduced to the facile assumption that history is only available in the form of pastiche or kitsch, as is evident in the 'heritage industry' and 'postmodern irony' alike. In this context, the past ceases to be another country, intriguing and challenging, waiting to be visited and explored again, but becomes a colony of the present. Of course, Warner well knows – indeed, insists upon reminding us – that historiography is an activity of the here and now. But she wants still to be able to find a past that has not been appropriated, and to bring back from it reports of myths and marvels which can guide us in forming a future that is not just a perpetuation of the world we currently inhabit. This, surely, is an important insight of fiction such as *Indigo*, which is postmodernist by virtue of being a critique of that sterile contemporaneity which is often designated as 'postmodern'.

If she is to be aligned with postmodernism at all, then, it must be in the positive sense intended by the late philosopher Jean-François Lyotard, who looked to art to resist that contemporary loss of value which he calls 'eclectic' or 'junk postmodernism'. He objected vociferously to what he saw as 'the epoch of slackening', characterized by a spirit of 'anything goes'. For him, this involved not only a temporal appropriation, across eras, but also a spatial appropriation, across areas. That is to say, diverse cultural forms of the present, from far and wide, become reduced by an homogenizing entertainment industry: 'Eclecticism is the degree zero of contemporary general culture: one listens to reggae, watches a western, eats McDonald's food for lunch and local cuisine for dinner, wears Paris perfume in Tokyo and 'retro' clothes in Hong Kong; knowledge is a matter for TV games' (Lyotard, 76). He saw that ethos as dictated by the cynical motive of profit, which always incorporates and represses any desire for true liberation. As such, it embodies a debased, commodified version of the postmodern. A truly radical and responsible postmodernist art will see it as its task to counter it. We are surely entitled to align Warner with such a movement of resistance; and it is her emphasis on the possibility of change, evident in her latest two works as in her earliest, that we will perhaps want to emphasize.

If ours is an age of irony, then perhaps the real irony is that in this era, where so much is made of free expression, of consumer rights, of the pursuit of material wealth regardless of any limits, natural or otherwise, it is yet possible to be rendered imaginatively immobile. Indeed, the globalized culture which claims to pander to all desires actually limits and prescribes the possibilities open to people; it renders vital autonomy less and less likely. What the media refer to as 'postmodern' society is not genuinely pluralistic, but rather imposes a conformity of expression, reducing difference to the level of the trivial – a matter of whim, fashion or 'taste'. It is eclectic but empty, allusive but arid.

Warner, who is unequivocally a feminist, socialist and postcolonial writer, and who may with due reservation be described as the author of postmodernist fiction, has long been aware of the perils of such pervasive banality, which relies on the pretence of diversity; and she has managed to affirm creative plenitude in the face of such cultural impoverishment. For that which we accept too readily as postmodernism is merely cultural petrifaction. What she has long advocated, and what she has demonstrated as novelist and as mythographer, is a sense of the marvellous beyond the choice of banalities which constitutes globalized culture. In particular, she has demonstrated the radical potential of mythically inspired literature to discover a true identity – between men and women, between the native and the foreign, between ourselves and others – which does not override differences. For the beauty of mythmaking is that it is at its most generously universal when it is most faithfully particular to the culture from which it originates. In her vision, stories confirm a community of imagination by celebrating the individuality – the strangeness, the wonder – of life. It is thanks to writers like her that we can still believe in the power of myth, metaphor and metamorphosis to present us with the possibility of 'other worlds'.

Select Bibliography

WORKS BY MARINA WARNER

Novels

In a Dark Wood (London: Weidenfeld & Nicolson, 1977; repr. London: Vintage, 1992).
The Skating Party (London: Weidenfeld & Nicolson, 1982; repr. London: Vintage, 1992).
The Lost Father (London: Chatto & Windus, 1988; repr. London: Vintage, 1998).
Indigo, or Mapping the Waters (London: Chatto & Windus, 1992; repr. London: Vintage, 1993).
The Leto Bundle (London: Chatto & Windus, 2000).

Short stories

The Mermaids in the Basement (London: Chatto & Windus, 1993; repr. London: Vintage, 1994).
Murderers I Have Known, and other stories (London: Chatto & Windus, 2000).

Drama

The Legs of the Queen of Sheba (libretto, with music by Julian Grant), produced London, 1991.
Tell Me More (television play), BBC, 1991.
In the House of Crossed Desires (libretto, with music by John Woolrich) (London: Faber, 1996).

Criticism, cultural history, mythography, etc.

The Dragon Empress: The Life and Times of Tz'u-hsi, Empress Dowager of China (London: Weidenfeld & Nicolson, 1972; repr. London: Vintage, 1993).

Alone of All Her Sex: The Myth and Cult of the Virgin Mary (London: Weidenfeld & Nicolson, 1976; repr. London: Vintage, 2000).

Joan of Arc: The Image of Female Heroism (London: Weidenfeld & Nicolson, 1981; repr. London: Vintage, 1991).

Monuments and Maidens: The Allegory of the Female Form (London: Weidenfeld & Nicolson, 1985; repr. London: Vintage, 1996).

Into the Dangerous World (pamphlet) (London: Chatto & Windus, 1989).

From the Beast to the Blonde: On Fairy Tales and their Tellers (London: Chatto & Windus, 1994; repr. London: Vintage, 1995).

Managing Monsters: Six Myths of our Time: The 1994 Reith Lectures (London: Vintage, 1994).

The Inner Eye: Art Beyond the Visible (London: National Touring Exhibitions, 1996).

No Go the Bogeyman: Scaring, Lulling, and Making Mock (London: Chatto & Windus, 1998; repr. London: Vintage, 2000).

Fantastic Metamorphoses, Other Worlds: Ways of Telling the Self (Oxford: Oxford University Press, 2002).

Edited works

Wonder Tales: Six Stories of Enchantment (London: Chatto & Windus, 1994; repr. London: Vintage, 1996).

For children

The Crack in the Teacup: Britain in the Twentieth Century (London: Deutsch, 1979).

The Impossible Day (London: Methuen, 1981).

The Impossible Night (London: Methuen, 1981).

The Impossible Bath (London: Methuen, 1982).

The Impossible Rocket (London: Methuen, 1982).

The Wobbly Tooth (London: Deutsch, 1984).

Essays and articles

Included here are some of the more important uncollected pieces which have not been incorporated into Warner's longer non-fictional works. *Signs and Wonders: Essays in Literature and Culture*, (London: Chatto & Windus, 2003) contains a wealth of other material.

'A Few Thoughts about Europe and its Legacy', *PN Review*, 82 (November–December 1991), 15–17.

'The Uses of Enchantment' (lecture at the National Film Theatre, 7 February 1992), in Duncan Petrie (ed.) *Cinema and the Realms of Enchantment* (London: British Film Institute Publishing, 1993), 13–

35.

'Rich Pickings', in Clare Boylan (ed.) *The Agony and the Ego: The Art and Strategy of Fiction Writing Explored*, (Harmondsworth: Penguin, 1993), 29–33.

'Angela Carter: Bottle Blonde, Double Drag', in Lorna Sage (ed.) *Flesh and the Mirror; Essays on the Art of Angela Carter*, (London: Virago Press, 1994), 243–56.

'The Structure of the Imagination: Darkness Visible in the Mind's Eye', in Wendy Pullan and Harshad Bhadeshia (eds) *Structure in Science and Art* (Cambridge: Cambridge University Press, 2000), 163–90.

INTERVIEWS WITH MARINA WARNER

Dabydeen, David, 'Marina Warner Interviewed', *Kunapipi*, 14:2 (1992), 115–23.

Kearney, Richard, 'Marina Warner: A European Woman's Heritage', *States of Mind: Dialogues with Contemporary Thinkers on the European Mind* (Manchester: Manchester University Press, 1995), 93–100.

Tredell, Nicolas, 'Marina Warner', *Conversations with Critics* (Manchester: Carcanet Press, 1994), 234–54.

Zabus, Chantal, 'Spinning a Yarn with Marina Warner', *Kunapipi*, 16:1 (1994), 519–29.

CRITICAL STUDIES AND BACKGROUND READING

Cakebread, Caroline, 'Sycorax Speaks: Marina Warner's *Indigo* and *The Tempest*', in Marianne Novy (ed.), *Transforming Shakespeare: Contemporary Women's Re-Visions in Literature and Performance* (New York: St Martin's Press, 1999), 217–35.

Connor, Steven, *The English Novel in History 1950–1995* (London: Routledge, 1996).

Coupe, Laurence, *Myth* (London: Routledge, 1997).

—— 'The Comedy of Terrors: Reading Myth with Marina Warner', *PN Review*, 128 (July–August 1999), 52–5.

Hutcheon, Linda, *A Poetics of Postmodernism: History, Theory and Fiction* (London: Routledge, 1988).

Kilian, Eveline, 'Visitations from the Past: The Fiction of Marina Warner', in Herausgegeben von Irmgard Maasson and Anna Maria Stuby (eds) *(Sub)Versions of Realism: Recent Women's Fiction in Britain* (Heidelberg: Universitätsverlag C. Winter, 1997), 55–69.

Todd, Richard, 'The Retrieval of Unheard Voices in British Postmodernist Fiction: A. S. Byatt and Marina Warner', in Theo D'Haen and

Hans Bertens (eds), *Liminal Postmodernisms: The Postmodern, the (Post-)Colonial and the (Post-)Feminist* (Amsterdam and Atlanta: Rodopi, 1994), 99–114.

—— *Consuming Fictions: The Booker Prize and Fiction in Britain Today* (London: Bloomsbury, 1996).

Zabus, Chantal, 'Prospero's Progeny Curses Back: Postcolonial, Postmodern and Postpatriarchal Rewritings of *The Tempest*', in Theo D'Haen and Hans Bertens (eds), *Liminal Postmodernism: The Postmodern, the (Post-)Colonial and the (Post-)Feminist* (Amsterdam and Atlanta: Rodopi, 1994), 115–39.

Index